Great Day Trips to Connecticut's Critical Habitats

Text & photographs by Robert Craig, Ph.D.

Paintings by Barbara Lussier

Road to Discovery Guides is an imprint of Perry Heights Press.

LCCN: 2004092523

ISBN 0-9630181-3-2

10 9 8 7 6 5 4 3 2 1

Contents

How To Use This Book 1

The idea of this volume is to discover. With a critical eye and critical thinking, some of the key ingredients necessary to conduct good science, the landscape of Connecticut reveals a depth of substance that escapes initial observation. Our region may not be singularly unique, but there is in it far more than we might presume. There is variety, and nuance, and infinite color and form.

I think of the Connecticut landscape more as I do the thoughtful paintings of the mature artist; not about stunning grandeur, but about looking inward at the simple elegance of its details: not Bierstadt's West, but the elderly Monet's garden. In his garden, Claude Monet focused on the familiar: the garden bridge, the cultivated flower, the shape of the pond lily. Through his vision he led us to discover them anew, and he educated us in the unexpected beauty of their subtlety.

The art that accompanies portions of this book is, in fact, present for reasons other than simply to decorate; it is there to assist in exploring this subtlety. Barbara Lussier has been drawing trees since she was six. The study of nature has always been a science and an art. For Barbara, painting Connecticut landscapes is about more than aesthetics; it is about watching life unfold. In the tradition of the Hudson River School, she draws inspiration from nature. Her work reminds us that natural places are critical not only because they sustain our lives, but also for the way they lift our souls.

This book has several purposes. Its fundamental one is to motivate a new generation of thinkers to venture into the field, with all of its discomforts and wonders, and to learn to a more perfect degree the workings of nature. Another is to stimulate students of nature and all who are thoughtful to appreciate the natural world as an aesthetic place with which we have an intimate connection. I will argue that it is through understanding this connection that we can formulate our most powerful arguments for its conservation.

Still one additional purpose of the book is to chronicle a personal and evolving perspective on the workings of the natural world. In order to accomplish this goal, I draw upon knowledge from not only our region, but from the totality of my experience, as it is this whole that has shaped my developing understanding. This personal perspective has lead to my formulating a new approach to conservation at the local level.

This is a new kind of guide to natural history. Its aim is to do more than simply describe hikes or walks and chronicle a list of what might be seen. It does these things, but it also provides insights into why the landscape is the way it is, and field trips have been chosen that help to bring such insights to life. Moreover, it explores the philosophy that forms, or should form, the underpinning of natural science and conservation. It does this by considering not only issues in biology, but the totality of human inquiry: the other natural sciences, mathematics, history, literature,

Artist Barbara Lussier created the paintings that accompany written descriptions of the habitats in this book. She is pictured with one of the Connecticut trees that inspire her work, an Eastern white pine.

and the arts. Chapters are thus divided into three broad although not entirely separate kinds of themes, or "lessons." These are considerations of natural science, of history, and of philosophy. My goal has been to provide by the last chapter tools for the thoughtful reader to use in developing a personal philosophy of the natural world.

In using this guide, I recommend that families and hiking companions first read and discuss the opening chapters together before making a trip. Afterwards, decide which habitat to visit and read and discuss that chapter. Go next to explore the habitats, and draw conclusions from the visit of what has been learned, and determine what new questions have arisen that require further exploration. Take along a field notebook and camera to keep a record of visits so that records can be compared against the chapter and referred to again before another visit. I have been making notes like this over 30 years, and I would now rank the volumes I have accumulated as my most valuable possession.

When making notes, for plants and invertebrates it is generally best to record scientific names, as the common names for these groups are not well standardized. I have followed this practice in the field trip chapters that follow, and use for the most part the nomenclature found in Gleason and Cronquist's *Manual of Vascular*

Plants of the Northeastern United States and Adjacent Canada for plant names, and Smith's *Key to Marine Invertebrates of the Wood's Hole Region* for invertebrate names. For amphibians, reptiles, birds and mammals, common names are fairly standardized, so I use only these, and I find that these are sufficient for taking notes on these groups.

I will begin this book by examining the major ecological subdivisions of the state, which have been called ecoregions. Within these ecoregions there are notable types of habitats, which I refer to as "critical" habitats. I explore 16 of these, along with their distinctive communities of plants and animals, by means of describing field trips that may be taken to outstanding examples of each. One of the advantages of Connecticut being a small state is that all these habitats can be visited in day trips.

Because the term critical refers to a high degree of conservation importance, I describe as well conservation considerations about the critical habitats, and develop a fresh understanding of what such habitats are. I pay special attention to those species termed "endangered" within the habitats, examine why such species are endangered, and re-examine what the term endangered should mean.

I have been thinking about issues like critical habitats and endangered species for a long time. Much of what I write involves new approaches to these issues. However, new ideas do not simply arise from nothingness, but build upon one's own previous thinking, as well as on those of others. Isaac Newton did not simply invent calculus one day. He developed this "new" approach to mathematics by synthesizing his own experiences and tying them to thoughts about geometry that had their origins in antiquity. As I also did not simply wake up one morning with an idea of what critical habitats and endangered species were, I begin here with a brief history of where my thinking comes from. Putting these ideas into this context gives us a basis for more complete understanding.

Origins 2

It has become hard for me to remember a time when thoughts of natural systems did not fill my head. Yet as I think of my earliest ideas on these subjects now, I find it surprising that I ever should have even considered them at all.

At age 18 I had hardly ever been out of the gritty working class neighborhoods of metropolitan New York City. Initially, city life was all I knew about, not natural history. Yet, for whatever cosmic reason it is that brings us to find our abiding interest, I found that wildness was something I wished to understand. By haunting the library for information about a time before the city existed, and by exploring city streets for remnants of places that were once country lanes, I found I could locate every tree native to the Northeast.

Animals proved far more difficult to locate, but by staring at shade trees and backyard shrubs I discovered that even in the heart of the city a trickle of wild animals flowed through- everything from Red-tailed Hawks to Red-headed Woodpeckers. I had to know more about this wildness that had preceded our tenure on the land.

So, the interest was born, and it brought me to Connecticut where I would consider this concept of wildness. The natives may have thought Connecticut suburban, but to me it looked more like paradise. There were real country lanes, and woods, and ponds, and birds that I had only dreamed about seeing a year before. It was in this still pastoral landscape that I investigated the natural world further. It was at this time that I met Joseph Dowhan.

We were students, respectively, in animal ecology and plant taxonomy. I was finishing a master's degree; Joe was a doctoral student. He had heard I was good at identifying birds, so sought me out to see if I had a summer job. He needed a zoologist to help doing inventories of plants and animals around the state. Like me, he had grown up in the shadow of the Empire State Building. He knew about summertime swimming expeditions to the lifeless waters of Newark Bay and about breathing yellow air, so in ways more important than might be guessed we made a natural team.

Joe had been employed by the Connecticut Department of Environmental Protection to interact with the University of Connecticut. At the height of the Earth Day era of the early 1970s, pressure had been applied to states to develop some notion of the status of their species, and Joe had been charged with devising an approach to learning this. But he had a wider vision: not just to make a list of what was "endangered" within the political limits of a state, but to place this endangered concept within the greater view of habitats and ecosystems. It was a novel and substantive approach, and it proved to set a standard for all states. He and his new idea would greatly influence and alter my thinking.

Upper Island, Lyme

So with that germ of an idea, the first modern survey of Connecticut's biota was born, and with it my first real focus on the subjects of critical habitats and endangered species. To be sure, we were both naïve and undereducated for the task at hand, but the vision was a sound starting point and we moved ahead with it. Like so many government initiatives, it easily could have dissipated into a summer romp in the woods, but we knew even then that we had the opportunity to make history. We were entering uncharted ground, and approached the task with a sense of urgency born from our limited life experiences: we *knew* what the world would be if the natural part of it were ignored. We knew as well that the history we made would be imperfect, and that it would remain for another time to evolve these initial ideas further.

Indeed, many of the issues raised in this volume are the direct descendants of ideas discussed around campfires during that first summer 28 years ago. We were aware that there were weaknesses with the concept of locally endangered species, and we knew also that any attempt to rank the importance of habitats and species would be a philosophical minefield. Yet we proceeded, and produced the first attempt at developing a comprehensive approach toward identifying and conserving the biological resources of our region.

I have said in classrooms a thousand times that philosophy

and science are not separate disciplines, but simply different aspects of the same inquiry. I point out that Aristotle and Descartes and even Einstein were all philosophers of science. It is why the terminal degree in science is called the Doctor of Philosophy. Since the initial appearance of our *Rare and Endangered Species of Connecticut and Their Habitats* in 1976, there has never been a comprehensive philosophical revision of that initial work. There has been tinkering with details, but no real rethinking of the underlying issues. In fact, an endangered species bureaucracy has evolved that helps to ensure the status quo. But bureaucracy is not science, and science can proceed only with continued self-examination and questioning of established dogma. In this volume I begin the process of revision, but before I do, I first provide an overview of topics to be covered.

The Language of Ecology 3

S cience has a language all its own. Mathematics is a key
component of this language and underlies much of what I
write here, although most readers will be relieved to know
that mathematics will not be discussed explicitly. In many senses
this is unfortunate, because to truly understand much of science
one must appreciate mathematics.

It is rather like a story told about Beethoven. A member
of his audience once asked him after a piano performance if he
could explain what his music was about. He responded that he
certainly could, and then proceeded to sit at the piano and play the
composition again. That's what it was about.

To understand music, one must understand the abstractions of musical form. To truly understand science, one must understand the abstractions of its language: mathematics.

The language of science is also one of philosophy. And, to expand on my earlier statement, science, philosophy and mathematics are all intimately related. You may remember that Rene Descartes wrote, "I think, therefore I am." But he also developed the Cartesian plane (the theory of graphing numbers), upon which much of advanced mathematics is based.

Pratt Cove, Deep River

In fact, without the mathematical philosophies of other individuals like Gottfried Leibnitz and Isaac Newton, who developed what is called the calculus, none of the analyses upon which key parts of this book are based would have been possible. As with any carefully crafted philosophy, a considered definition of terms is necessary.

Endangered species: species that are in danger of extinction. They may be undergoing long term population declines that are not part of normal population fluctuations. They also may be species that have stable populations, but ones that are persistently low, making them extremely sensitive to environmental alteration. Endangered species are generally threatened by some agent of decline, like habitat loss, environmental pollution, or overharvesting. The term can refer to the status of species throughout their range (in danger of complete extinction) or to populations in a particular geographic region (in danger of regional extirpation). However, in the latter case a number of factors other than simply population status enter into consideration. I will discuss such considerations under a separate heading.

Community: In years past, ecologists frequently used this term to signify the presence of a group of tightly integrated, interacting species. Because natural groupings of species do not necessarily interact extensively, a more general definition is now often used. Such a definition might simply state that a community is a group of species occurring at a geographic location within a particular type of habitat. Ecologists also refer to communities of specific types of organisms, such as forest tree communities, forest bird communities and forest insect communities. However, all such definitions, as well as those that follow, represent attempts at categorizing what is in reality a natural continuum. As I discuss in Chapter 4, such categorizing has useful purposes, but it also has limitations.

Ecoregion: We may define the term ecoregion as referring to a major geographic location that is characterized by distinctive topography, climate and, consequently, natural communities. Because nature is in reality a continuum, subdividing the landscape into separate regions is a subjective decision. So, I argue in Chapter 4 that we must determine what is distinctive based on what will provide tools useful for understanding the role of ecological processes in shaping patterns observed in nature.

Critical habitat: Habitats are natural places where living organisms carry on biological processes. They are critical ones when they serve some fundamental ecological role and, hence, are of key conservation importance. As originally defined, this term referred principally to rarely occurring habitats in which rare species occurred. However, I will argue in Chapter 5 that a more inclusive definition is required. I define them as not solely rare habitats but common ones as well, as it is within the commonly occurring habitats that most of the region's biological diversity may be found. Moreover, it is within these common habitats that the vast majority of crucial ecological processes occur; phenomena like primary production, nutrient cycling and population dynamics.

The Ecoregions of Connecticut 4

Humans seem to have a need to categorize. It is a need that by and large serves us well, although within the realm of science it can lead to conflict. But like others, scientists have always attempted to categorize nature.

We see the hand of the categorizer even in the scientists of antiquity: Aristarchus, Lucretius, and even Virgil, who took time out from writing epic poems to consider the structure of nature. We indeed owe much of our present view of the biological world to the greatest categorizer of all, Carolus Linnaeus, who in the 18th century devised a system to classify species.

But even Linnaeus' seminal attempts at classifying illustrate the limitations of such efforts. What determines where we draw the line as to what species are? What do you do when species hybridize rampantly, like many plants do? How should we view populations that appear and act like species, but in terms of their makeup also could be classified as genetic aberrations, like certain salamanders?

Such problems with categorizing have been around since the beginnings of Ecology as well. Early ecologists, for example, devised elaborate protocols for distinguishing separate plant communities. But then other ecologists stated the obvious: nature was a continuum. Communities blended from one to another. They were not necessarily distinct, tightly integrated and interacting groups of species with characteristics of some "superorganism". They often could be described as simply collections of species occurring together because their ranges of habitat needs overlapped.

But still, because doing so serves useful purposes, categorizing continues in Ecology. The concept of community may have evolved over the decades, but it remains a powerful theme in ecological investigations. Similarly, the landscape classification scheme referred to as the ecoregion concept is a venerable and enduring one. Its origins may be traced in part to an individual with strong Connecticut connections: C. Hart Merriam, who in 1877 penned the first comprehensive distributional analysis of Connecticut birds. In 1899 he also developed the notion of life zones.

This life zone concept figured prominently in the 1913 Birds of Connecticut. Bird life across much of Connecticut was described as being characteristic of the Alleghenian zone, whereas coastal birds were said to have Carolinian (Southeastern) affinities. The species of the northernmost parts of Connecticut showed an affiliation with the Canadian zone, because they were more characteristic of these northern regions. Thus was born the tradition of thinking about natural subdivisions occurring in the Connecticut landscape.

Even today, Merriam's categories remain a more substantive concept than many modern ecologists recognize.

To be sure, the term ecoregion was coined much later. It was first used in 1962 to define the major forest regions of maritime Canada. We may define ecoregion as referring to geographic locations that are characterized by a distinctive topography, climate and, consequently, natural communities. The trick is in deciding what distinctive is. The decision, as in much of categorizing, is a subjective one. Moreover, it is one that may be influenced by what one is interested in finding. Ideally, the definition should be one that yields tools useful for understanding patterns and processes in nature. In the sections that follow, examples will demonstrate that the concept can indeed satisfy such criteria, especially where quantitative data can be brought to bear in making decisions.

In *Rare and Endangered Species of Connecticut and Their Habitats*, five principal ecological zones with 15 ecoregions were identified based on topography, geology, regional climate, prevailing life forms, and presence of rare "indicator" species. Because the boundaries of the regions subdivide what is in reality an environmental gradient, their exact placement may be argued. Moreover, the degree of ecoregion distinctness is in part a function of which physical factors or groups of organisms one examines. Again, however, the key issue is not precise boundary placement, but whether the delineation of such regions assists with identifying important natural phenomena.

In order to facilitate identifying such phenomena, I depart in several ways from the original designations. When comparing regional attributes, lumping similar categories helps with strengthening the power of analyses (through things like statistical tests), so I choose to simplify the ecoregion scheme and more specifically separate topographically distinct regions. To help accomplish the simplification, I adopt a view more like that used for defining biomes (major geographic regions of the world with similar vegetation types): the prevailing vegetation rather than rare species at range limits (rare "indicator" species) define the region. When we use the environmental gradient approach to ecology, it becomes clear that species at their range limit may be found anywhere. The presence of species at such limits may provide verification of ecological distinctions, but they themselves appear insufficient for defining regions. Shifts in overall vegetation patterns seem much more likely to reveal major ecological distinctions than presence of several rare species.

By using such criteria, I redefine the ecoregions of Connecticut as consisting of eight. I justify further these designations and detail the characteristics of the new ecoregions below.

The Ecoregions

Northern Uplands zone

The northern uplands consist of those regions where the highest elevations and greatest relief are found. The zone may be divided into two geographically separate regions in northeast and northwest Connecticut.

a. Northwest Uplands Ecoregion: Topographic features do not end at state boundaries, so if we view the Berkshire Plateau as a whole, the northwest corner of Connecticut appears comparatively uniform in types of natural communities present. The next substantive distinctions in forest types are found further north in places like the Adirondack, Green and White Mountains, and to a lesser degree the Berkshire Mountains of Massachusetts. These regions exhibit a much more pervasive shift from oak-dominated forests to those in which Sugar Maple, Yellow Birch, American Beech, Eastern Hemlock and Eastern White Pine (northern hardwoods-hemlock-white pine) dominate the landscape. Such forest associations certainly occur in more moist areas in extreme northwestern Connecticut, but they occur as well south throughout Litchfield County. Even on the slopes of the highest peaks in the region, I have found on east, west, and north-facing slopes that forests dominated by trees like Northern Red, White, Scarlet, Chestnut and Black Oak are also widespread. The abundant presence on the highest elevations of species like Scrub Oak, Sassafras, Black Oak and Pitch Pine, characteristic also of Connecticut coastal areas, argues that this region is not in a truly (physiologically?) distinctive bio-climatic zone.

Previously, the highest elevations of Northwest Connecticut were separated into a distinct region, the Northwest Highlands Ecoregion. Although

Lake Zoar, Southbury

areas of greatest elevation do indeed harbor some herbaceous plants like Mountain Wood-sorrel that are near their southern range limit, the same could be said for any region. Hence, pending a more complete quantitative assessment of prevailing forest cover in these areas, I presently judge the entire region as better considered a single zone, the Northwest Upland Ecoregion.

The Northwest Uplands exhibit considerable topographic relief. Elevations are generally above 600 feet, although they descend below 500 feet along the Housatonic River. They reach a maximum of 2,380 feet at the summit of Bear Mountain in Salisbury. Geologically, crystalline rocks such as metamorphic gneisses and schists characterize much of the region, although deposits of marble also are present. Some of the state's better agricultural soils develop in marble regions. Climatically, the region is in plant hardiness zone five. Its mean annual temperature is 47°F, annual precipitation may be as much as 50 inches, and it is on average characterized by the coldest and snowiest (60 or more inches/year) winters in Connecticut.

The prevailing flora includes those oak-dominated and northern hardwoods-hemlock-white pine types mentioned above. In coves, Eastern Hemlock can form nearly pure coniferous stands or co-occur with Eastern White Pine. Eastern White Pine is often a dominant tree species in forests, particularly where it has heavily seeded in after a disturbance such as logging. On drier sites, Scarlet and Chestnut Oak are common. Black Spruce bogs are also present at some locations.

b. Northeast Uplands Ecoregion: Much like the Northwest Uplands, from which it is separated by the Connecticut River Valley, the Northeast Uplands is characterized by considerable topographic relief. The principal difference is that the extent of the region is dramatically less than the Northwest Uplands. Elevations are generally above 600 feet, and reach a maximum of 1,315 feet on Burley Hill in Union. Geologically, crystalline rocks such as metamorphic gneisses and schists typify much of the region. Climatically, the region is in plant hardiness zone five. Its mean annual temperature is 47°F, annual precipitation is 43 inches, and it has winters similarly cold and snowy (60 inches/year) to the Northwest Hills.

The prevailing flora is also similar to that of the Northwest Uplands, and includes oak-dominated and northern hardwoods-hemlock-white pine forest. In coves, Eastern Hemlock may predominate or co-occur with Eastern White Pine. Eastern White Pine is often a dominant tree species in forests, particularly where it has heavily seeded in after a disturbance. On drier sites, Scarlet and Chestnut Oak are common. Black Spruce bogs are also present at some locations.

From 60 sampling stations in the Northeast Uplands, I found

that this ecoregion had substantially greater cover by conifer and northern hardwoods-conifer forest, and substantially less cover by oak-dominated and dry pine-oak forest than more southern portions of eastern Connecticut.

Northern Hills zone

These more gently rolling hills are present south of the Northern Uplands, and are again separated into two geographically separate regions.

a. Northwest Hills Ecoregion: Hilly terrain with elevations ranging from under 250 feet in river valleys to 1,200 feet on ridges characterizes the area. Geologically, it is similar to the Northwest Uplands, with schist, gneiss and smaller areas of marble present. Climatically, it is in plant hardiness zone six during many but not all winters. Mean annual temperature is 48°F, annual precipitation is 45 inches, and snowfall averages 50 inches.

The prevailing flora is oak-dominated forest, in which Red Maple, Black Birch and various species of hickories are common associates. In drier areas, Eastern White Pine and Pitch Pine frequently occur with oaks, particularly Black, Scarlet and Chestnut Oak. More diverse associations that include species like Yellow Poplar, White Ash, Sugar Maple, Northern Red Oak and Yellow Birch are typical at moister sites. In coves, Eastern Hemlock may predominate or co-occur with Eastern White Pine. Eastern White Pine also may predominate locally in various situations where it has seeded in heavily after a disturbance. Black Spruce bogs are present locally as well.

b. Northeast Hills Ecoregion: Hilly terrain with elevations ranging from under 150 feet in river valleys to over 1,000 feet on ridges characterizes the area. Geologically, metamorphic schists and gneisses predominate. Climatically, it is in plant hardiness zone six during many, but not all winters. Mean annual temperature is 48°F, annual precipitation averages 44 inches and snowfall averages 50 inches.

Much like the Northwest Hills, the prevailing flora is oak-dominated forest, in which Red Maple, Black Birch and various species of hickories are common associates. In drier areas, Eastern White Pine and Pitch Pine frequently associate with oaks, particularly Black, Scarlet and Chestnut Oak. More diverse forest communities that include species like Yellow Poplar, White Ash, Sugar Maple, Northern Red Oak and Yellow Birch are typical at moister sites. In coves, Eastern Hemlock may

Talcott Mountain, Bloomfield

predominate or co-occur with Eastern White Pine. Eastern White Pine also may predominate locally in various situations where it has seeded in heavily after a disturbance. In swamps, Atlantic White Cedar may be common to dominant, although Black Spruce occurs occasionally as well, particularly in bogs.

From 330 sampling stations in the Northeast Hills, I found that this ecoregion had substantially lower cover by conifer and northern hardwoods-conifer forest, and substantially more cover by oak-dominated and dry pine-oak forest than in the Northeast Uplands. However, it had less oak forest and more conifer-dominated forest communities than in areas to the south.

Southern Hills zone

The lower hills of southern Connecticut receive greater climatic modification from the proximity of Long Island Sound than do areas further to the north. They may be divided into two geographically separate regions.

a. Southwest Hills Ecoregion: Hilly terrain with elevations ranging from about 100 feet in river valleys to nearly 1,000 feet on ridges characterizes the area. Geologically, metamorphic schists and gneisses typify it, although limited areas of marble occur in valleys. Climatically, it is firmly in plant hardiness zone six. Mean annual temperature is 49.5°F, precipitation is 45 inches, and snowfall averages 40 inches.

Much like the Northwest Hills, the prevailing flora is oak-dominated forest, in which Red Maple, Black Birch and various species of hickories are common associates. In drier areas, Eastern White Pine and Pitch Pine frequently associate with oaks, particularly Black, Scarlet and Chestnut Oak. More diverse forest communities that include species like Yellow Poplar, White Ash, Sugar Maple, Northern Red Oak and Yellow Birch are typical at moister sites. In coves, Eastern Hemlock may predominate or co-occur with Eastern White Pine. However, areas dominated by conifers are less frequent than in more northern areas, and Eastern White Pine becomes a progressively less frequent species toward the coast. Eastern Redcedar is a more abundant successional species than Eastern White Pine in the region.

b. Southeast Hills Ecoregion: Hilly terrain with elevations ranging from under 50 feet in river valleys to nearly 800 feet on ridges characterizes the area. Geologically, metamorphic schists and gneisses typify it.   Climatically, it is firmly in plant hardiness zone six.   Mean annual temperature is 49°F, annual precipitation is 45 inches, and snowfall averages 40 inches.

Much like the Northeast Hills, the prevailing flora is oak-dominated forest, in which Red Maple, Black Birch and various species of hickories are common associates. In drier areas, Eastern White Pine and Pitch Pine frequently associate with oaks, particularly Black, Scarlet and Chestnut Oak. Such associations are widespread near the Rhode Island border, where glacial sand and gravel deposits favor their development. More diverse forest communities that include species like Yellow Poplar, White Ash, Sugar Maple, Northern Red Oak and Yellow Birch are typical at moister sites.

In coves, Eastern Hemlock may predominate or co-occur with Eastern White Pine. However, areas dominated by conifers are less frequent than in more northern areas, and Eastern White Pine becomes progressively less frequent toward the coast. Eastern Redcedar is a more abundant successional species than Eastern White Pine in the region. In swamps, Atlantic White-cedar may be common to abundant. From 330 sampling stations in the Southeast Hills, I found that this ecoregion had more cover by oak-dominated forest but less cover by conifer-containing communities than in areas to the north.

Central Lowlands zone

The upper Connecticut River Valley comprises this zone. Where the Connecticut River turns into the Southeast Hills at Middletown, the Central Lowlands turn west and continue south to New Haven. Much of upper region was a glacial lake during the close of the glacial era.

Central Lowlands Ecoregion: Sedimentary sandstones characterize this geologically distinct region, although traprock (basalt) ridges of ancient volcanic origin run north south through the region. Elevations are generally below 250 feet, but may reach nearly 1,000 feet on ridges. Climatically, it is firmly within plant hardiness zone six. Mean annual temperature is 50°F, annual precipitation is 45 inches, and snowfall averages 44 inches.

The prevailing flora is oak-dominated forest, in which Red Maple, Black Birch and various species of hickories are common associates. In drier areas, Eastern White Pine and Pitch Pine frequently associate with oaks, particularly Black, Scarlet and Chestnut Oak. Pitch Pine may come to predominate in disturbed spots where glacial sand and gravel deposits favor its growth. In moister sites, more diverse forest communities that include species like Yellow Poplar, White Ash, Sugar Maple, Northern Red Oak and Yellow Birch are typical. Moreover, especially along the Connecticut River and its major tributaries, extensive areas are vegetated by floodplain forest, in which species like Eastern Cottonwood, Silver Maple, Green Ash, Bitternut Hickory and Pin Oak are common. In coves, particularly on traprock ridges, Eastern Hemlock may predominate or co-occur with Eastern White Pine. Eastern Redcedar is often an important successional species in old fields.

Coastal zone

Coastal Ecoregion: Gneiss, schist and granite, as well as some sandstone characterize this region. Modest deposits of current and wind-carried sand also occur, and form islands and sand spits near the mouths of some rivers. Elevations are generally below 250 feet. Climatically, it has a mean annual temperature of 51°F, and borders being in plant hardiness zone seven. Mean annual precipitation is 45 inches, and snowfall averages less than 35 inches.

The prevailing flora is oak-dominated forest, in which species like Black, Scarlet and White Oak co-occur with Mockernut Hickory, Sassafras, Black Cherry and Red Maple. Conifers make up a comparatively infrequent component of coastal forests, although Pitch Pine is locally common. Forests are also frequently more open in character, due in part to mechanical damage incurred during coastal storms. These more open areas are generally densely overgrown with vine species like Catbriar. Eastern Redcedar is often an important successional species in old fields. From 45 sample stations in this region, I determined that forests were overwhelmingly oak-dominated, and had nominal cover by conifer-containing communities.

In addition to forest habitats, tidal wetlands occur along the coast and up rivers, with salt marsh and cattail marsh being the principal marsh habitats. In sites most exposed to salt spray and mechanical damage from wind and waves, scrub thickets with species like High Tide Bush, Groundsel Tree and Beach Plum replace forest.

Although this region was in *Rare and Endangered Species of Connecticut and Their Habitats* described as extending several miles inland, based on direct field observations I conclude that the principal influence of coastal environments on forest communities extends inland about one mile. It also extends up major rivers to the limit of salt water intrusion. Beyond this distance, forests are virtually indistinguishable from those of the Southern Hills zone. Hence, I define the Coastal Ecoregion as being only that area nearest the sea.

Ecoregions & distributional patterns

As I stated in the introduction to this topic, the utility of the ecoregion concept is in its ability to help clarify the processes that produce patterns observed in nature. Data on bird population densities from eastern Connecticut illustrate the occurrence of patterns that are coincident with ecoregion boundaries, and examination of habitats used by these birds provides insights into the reason for these distributions.

For example, the Winter Wren is at its southern range limit in Connecticut, where it inhabits especially the conifer-dominated swamps prevalent in the Northeast Uplands. Summer densities of the Winter Wren are greatest in the Northeast Uplands Ecoregion.

Similarly, the Black-throated Blue Warbler approaches its southern range limit in Connecticut, where it occupies habitats (northern hardwoods-conifer forests with dense understories of Mountain Laurel) found most frequently in the Northeast Uplands. Summer densities of the Black-throated Blue Warbler are greatest in the Northeast Uplands Ecoregion.

Winter Wren summer density in eastern Connecticut. Light areas indicate low density, dark areas higher density.

Black-throated Blue Warbler summer density in eastern Connecticut. Light areas indicate low density, dark areas higher density.

In contrast, the Red-eyed Vireo has a center of abundance in the Southeast Hills, where it is particularly abundant in the oak-dominated forests that prevail in the region. Summer densities of the Red-eyed Vireo are greatest in Southeast Connecticut.

Red-eyed Vireo summer density in eastern Connecticut. Light areas indicate low density, gray areas mid-range density, dark areas higher density.

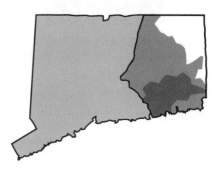

The American Redstart, which has declined over areas of the Northeast as forests have matured, is now found particularly near the coast. It is associated with forest openings and younger forest, and such habitats are frequent near the coast. Greatest densities of the American Redstart are concentrated along the Connecticut shoreline.

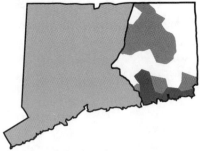

American Redstart summer density in eastern Connecticut. Light areas indicate low density, gray areas mid-range density, dark areas high density.

Still other species use ecoregions differently depending on the season. For example, the more southerly distributed Tufted Titmouse is widespread across eastern Connecticut in summer (although note its lack of occurrence in the Northeast Uplands!), but its winter populations predominate in the Southeast Hills.

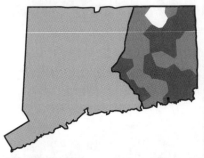

The Tufted Titmouse is widespread in eastern Connecticut in summer.

The milder climate of the Southeast Hills during this energetically expensive season (i.e. it takes a lot of calories to stay warm on a winter day) is likely responsible for this population shift in a species more at home in Southeastern North America.

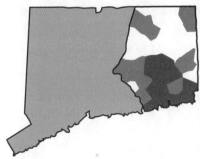

Titmouse winter densities were greatest in southeast Connecticut.

Critical Habitats of Connecticut 5

Wwhat makes a natural habitat critical? We might think of a critical habitat in a general way as an area of key conservation importance, but as with much of science, the complete answer is less straightforward than we might hope. In years past, such places have been characterized also as rare habitats or places where concentrations of endangered species occur. At first glance criteria like these seem reasonable enough, but in practice the logic behind them has on occasion become circular: critical habitats are defined as places where endangered species concentrate, and species are defined as endangered because they occupy critical habitats.

And this brings up a key related issue: which species are properly called endangered? We will return to that rather thorny question later. For now, let us focus on defining critical habitats.

I would argue that critical habitats are more than simply unusual places or places where endangered species are found. They also are those places critical for keeping our major natural processes operating. They are the ones responsible for maintaining such system attributes as biodiversity, and system processes like nutrient cycles and productivity. The really critical habitats are also those we take for granted: the common ones.

We have sometimes assumed that these common habitats are secure, so we can focus on the rare ones. But we do so with little evidence to support this sense of security. In part this weak evidence is a consequence of the situation being more complex than considering only individual habitats. Habitats are components of larger ecological systems. Even if a thousand acres of some habitat are protected, the system of which it is a part is not necessarily secure.

Let us consider these ideas in light of some real data. My observations on Connecticut forest bird distributions show that not even the most common species are distributed uniformly. Even the phenomenally abundant Red-eyed Vireo is plentiful only in certain geographic regions. If we return to the map of its distribution in eastern Connecticut (Chapter 4), the species is comparatively infrequent in the northeastern corner of the state, and most common toward its southeastern corner.

So why might this be? Because I concurrently collected information on habitats while doing population surveys, it became clear that Red-eyed Vireos favored oak-dominated forest- a common local habitat- particularly in southern Connecticut where population densities were greatest. So, even though oak forest may not be the sort of place that makes conservationists wax poetic, for the Red-eyed Vireo it is the greatest thing since chocolate ice cream. In fact, this species is just one of a number I found to focus on oak-dominated forest. The habitat is certainly a major contributor toward sustaining regional biodiversity.

My study also made it clear that what we refer to as our regional forest bird community is actually a highly heterogeneous collection of species that requires a variety of habitat types within the forest landscape. I identified species to be associated with such habitat classes as 1) extensive, unbroken tracts of mature forest (e.g. Pileated Woodpecker), 2) young forest (e.g. Yellow-billed Cuckoo), 3) open canopy forest (e.g. Gray Catbird), 4) places where forest trees had fallen, creating "forest gaps" (e.g. American Redstart), 5) mature conifer forest (e.g. Black-throated Green Warbler), young conifer forest (e.g. Magnolia Warbler), 7) deciduous forest (e.g. Red-eyed Vireo), 8) forests with dense understories (e.g. Eastern Towhee), 9) open canopy swamps (e.g. Common Yellowthroat), 10) closed canopy swamps (e.g. Northern Waterthrush), 11) riparian forest (e.g. Yellow-throated Vireo) and 12) pine-oak barrens (e.g. Prairie Warbler). Single species also could occupy more than one habitat type (e.g. Yellow-throated Vireo uses riparian forest and forest gaps). Moreover, permanent resident species changed their habitat use from summer to winter (e.g. Red-bellied Woodpecker). So, if this community is to persist in its entirety, a variety of habitats not traditionally thought of as critical must be protected, and we must consider ecological processes occurring at more than one season if we are to develop a meaningful conservation strategy.

In my studies, I focused on exploring only those areas large enough (minimum 250 acres) to permit establishment of one of my 2 mile-long survey transects. In practice, most areas studied had more than 1000 acres of contiguous forest. Despite investigating such extensive tracts, my data showed that no one tract supported the entire complement of forest bird species. Each tract had its own characteristics, which favored certain species and discouraged others. Hence, even protection of a large tract would be insufficient for preserving the entire forest bird community. Only a series of such tracts appear likely to ensure the long-term persistence of just our forest bird community.

In order to maintain all bird species within the larger forest ecosystem, at a minimum all of its habitat types must be represented in a list of critical habitats. Because the presence of particular habitats is in part a function of landscape features like elevation, slope, soil moisture, soil type and topography, the implication is also that tracts extensive enough to provide a variety of physical environments are required. Only extensive regions are likely to provide the range of physical variety necessary to support all species. Moreover, especially for those species existing at low densities, extensive tracts are essential for protecting populations large enough to be self-sustaining. So, a focus on critical habitats alone is insufficient for ensuring the persistence of biodiversity. A proper conservation approach preserves large tracts that include examples of a variety of critical habitats. In other words, habitats do not exist as discrete entities; they exist as features of larger ecosystems.

With this discussion as a starting point, we are now ready to explore this newly expanded world of critical habitats. As with any attempt to categorize the continuum of nature, a list of critical habitats has elements of the artificial associated with it, it exposes the biases of the categorizer (my bias is the perspective of a terrestrial vertebrate ecologist), and it focuses on terrestrial systems. A careful reader also will recognize that there are overlaps among these habitat categories, in part because habitats are often part of an environmental continuum rather than discrete entities.

CRITICAL HABITATS OF CONNECTICUT

As I have stated, habitats are natural places where living organisms carry on biological processes. They are critical ones when they serve some fundamental ecological role and, hence, are of key conservation importance. One can think of numerous examples of key ecological roles of habitats. Wetland habitats, for example, can have extremely high primary productivity (the rate at which living material is made), they can filter excess nutrients (e.g. nitrate and phosphate pollutants) from sediments and convert them into living material, and they can play an integral role in the water cycle. In Connecticut, the following critical habitats can be identified:

Oak-dominated forest:
The majority of Connecticut is forested (about 60 percent), and forest communities where oaks are key constituents are among the most widespread of natural habitats. They are particularly prevalent in the southern part of the state. Oaks do not exist in forests alone, but co-occur with species like hickories, Red Maple and birches. A wide variety of shrubs and herbaceous plants make their homes in these forests as well. These forests and other Connecticut forest types

Virgin Black Oak

have been maturing, and in many locations have begun to exhibit characteristics of old growth forests for the first time since the 17th century. Roughly 100 species of birds can occur in oak-dominated forests during the course of the year, along with forest-dwelling amphibians, reptiles and mammals. The number of invertebrate species (like insects, snails and spiders) present in them is immense.

Mixed deciduous forest: As soil conditions become moister and richer, such as at the bottom of hills or in protected sites, oak-dominated forests give way to ones where maples, birches, ashes and a variety of other tree species become common. This is not to say that oaks and hickories are absent (although species like Scarlet and Chestnut Oak disappear), but they become less important. As with oak forests, a wide variety of vertebrate and invertebrate species are present, although as pointed out before, individual species may occupy this habitat at densities different from those in other forest habitats.

Conifer-northern hardwood forest: Across northern Connecticut, particularly in the higher relief areas of the northwestern and extreme northeastern parts of the state, the deciduous forests give way to ones where conifers become much more important constituents. Eastern White Pine, Eastern Hemlock, Sugar Maple, American Beech, Northern Red Oak and Yellow Birch are among the common trees of this habitat. Earlier authors have separated this habitat into two components, a conifer-transition hardwood forest and a conifer-northern hardwoods zone, but I choose to combine these, as they are not sufficiently different in our region to warrant separation. Moreover, as with ecoregions, statistical considerations argue for combining such similar categories in order to facilitate comparative analyses.

Animal species more characteristic of northern New England, and found infrequently or not at all in oak-dominated forests, are regular inhabitants of these forests. Some of these species, like the Dark-eyed Junco, Black-throated Blue Warbler and Northern Flying Squirrel reach their southern range limit in conifer-northern hardwood forests.

Pine-oak forest: In neighboring Massachusetts, Rhode Island, Long Island and New Jersey there are extensive and outstanding examples of this habitat. It is less well developed in Connecticut, although it is found in dry, gravelly and sandy soils throughout the state. Eastern White Pine-oak forest occurs most frequently, although Pitch Pine may co-occur with these species. Pitch Pine occasionally assumes a dominant role in pine-oak forests, particularly in areas along the Rhode Island border and in spots in the Connecticut Valley. Certain animal species find this habitat type particularly appealing, notably the Fowler's Toad, Eastern Hognose Snake and Eastern Towhee.

Conifer forest: Naturally occurring conifer forest is found in

Connecticut particularly in coves along streams. Such forests can be composed of nearly pure Eastern Hemlock or a combination of hemlock and Eastern White Pine. However, naturally occurring stands of Eastern White Pine also occur fairly commonly, especially in northern Connecticut. Eastern White Pine reproduces vigorously in disturbed areas, and as it matures it can become the overwhelmingly dominant tree species in certain locations. Our most rare conifer habitat is native Red Spruce forest, which is found at a few small locations in Northwest Connecticut. The animal life of conifer forests is rather distinctive, and includes species like the Red Squirrel, Blackburnian Warbler, and Red-breasted Nuthatch.

Coastal woodland and scrub: Although not nearly as distinctive and well developed as they are in neighboring Massachusetts, New Jersey and Long Island, in part because of overwhelming shoreline development, fine examples of these habitats are still present on the Connecticut coast. They show distinctive development because Long Island Sound moderates coastal climates and coastal storms damage trees. Such tree species as Black Oak, Sassafras and Bitternut Hickory are particularly prevalent near the coast. Catbriar and similar vines can form an impenetrable understory in them.

In the most exposed locations, wind and salt spray can stunt vegetation to the point where coastal scrub thickets replace forests. More typically southern species like Post Oak may be found in such locations, along with salt tolerant coastal specialist shrubs like Beach Plum and High Tide Bush.

Riparian habitats: Areas along our larger rivers form natural breaks in the forest canopy, and due to their generally moister, richer physical environments, and to the mechanical damage caused in them by periodic flooding and uprooting of trees, they develop into distinctive habitats. Forest canopies in such areas may be comparatively open, and they are vegetated by a characteristic flora of woody and herbaceous plants.

Floodplain habitats develop where comparatively flat topography borders a river. They are periodically inundated with floodwaters, most notably during spring snowmelt. Of Connecticut's habitats, they are among the most aesthetic, being graced with such forms as the multi-trunked Silver Maple and the gaunt, skeletal Pin Oak. In the rich and wet soils of the floodplain, mature specimens of these and other trees like American Sycamore trees reach titanic proportions. Moreover, the understory of forests may be carpeted in spring with profusion of wildflowers, and in summer with an often dense and distinctive herbaceous flora. Aquatic and semi-aquatic mammals like the Beaver, River Otter and Mink can all be found frequenting these habitats. Bird species like the Yellow-throated Vireo and Northern Oriole find such habitats particularly appealing.

Tidal marshes: Marshes are places vegetated with herbaceous plants like grasses and sedges. Tidal marshes are those exposed to tidal action. Along the coast where water salinity and tidal action are greatest, distinctive types called salt marshes develop. They are dominated by several species of salt grass, and along their upper reaches by a dark species of rush called Black Grass. The animal life is as distinctive as the plant life, and includes species like the Seaside Sparrow and Clapper Rail.

As the influence of water salinity and tides declines along tidal rivers, salt marshes are progressively replaced by brackish Narrow-leaved Cattail marshes and ultimately freshwater tidal marshes. These freshwater communities have a rather more diverse flora in which River Bulrush, Water Horsetail, Wild Rice and Tuckahoe are among the most abundant species. Freshwater tidal marshes are characterized by species like the Swamp Sparrow and Virginia Rail.

Freshwater marshes and shrub swamps: Non-tidal freshwater marshes are similar to tidal ones in being primarily herbaceous, although other plants species like Broad-leaved Cattail, Tussock Sedge, Umbrella Sedge and Water Lily are often most abundant.

Freshwater marshes also may intergrade with wetland-associated shrubs like Buttonball Bush, Highbush Blueberry and Winterberry. Where shrubs become dominant, these communities are called shrub swamps. The animal life of these habitats includes species like the Eastern Ribbon Snake, Musk Turtle and Northern Water Snake.

Swamps: Low, poorly drained locations develop into several distinctive forest communities in Connecticut. Because trees growing in waterlogged soil are often weakly rooted, trees may fall over, leaving the forest canopy partially open. The most typical swamps are those dominated by Red Maple, although more diverse deciduous communities with Yellow Birch, Green Ash, Black Ash and Swamp White Oak also may be found. In addition, Eastern White Pine and Eastern Hemlock can invade swamps to form mixed cover associations. Sometimes the coniferous Atlantic White-cedar occurs with them, particularly in eastern Connecticut. This species can become dominant in swamps after disturbance, and such places are referred to as white-cedar swamps. All have dense understories vegetated by shrubs like Winterberry (a species of holly) and Sweet Pepperbush. Swamp specialist animals include the Red-backed Vole, Water Shrew, and Northern Waterthrush.

Bogs: Like swamps, bogs are wet places, although their origin is rather different. Many can trace their origins to glacial times, as they have developed in water-filled depressions left by melting blocks of glacial ice (a glacial kettle hole). Unlike most habitats in which the physical environment determines the biotic one, in this instance biological processes are involved in creating the environment. Bogs characteristically develop as plants colonize around the edge of a pond. Some kinds of plants, notably sedges, extend in mats from the edge over the pond surface. These mats accumulate dead plant remains and rain them into the acidic, low nutrient and low oxygen environment of the pond. Over time, the detritus accumulates into a thick organic layer called peat. Older portions of the bog are progressively colonized by low shrubs like Leatherleaf and then by trees like Black Spruce and Tamarack. Hence, younger bogs have a marshy appearance, whereas old bogs may be forested. Old New England bogs are often called Black Spruce bogs.

Beaches: As with coastal scrub, our poorly developed beaches in Connecticut are a far cry from the spectacular beach environments of Cape Cod, Long Island, and coastal New Jersey. However, they are still a widespread coastal habitat. Moreover, even our small beaches are home to a distinctive flora and fauna, and serve as host to some of the region's most genuinely endangered species. Connecticut beaches are of two general classes; sand spits (sand deposits projecting out from the upland) and upland-Sound fringe beaches. Sand spits can become detached from the upland to form island beaches, although in Long Island Sound they never develop into the extensive barrier islands seen on Long Island. The most widespread and common beach plant is Dune Grass, which is integrally responsible for stabilizing sand dunes. A small variety of other peculiarly adapted plant species like Sea Rocket and Beach Pea vegetate beaches as well. Animal life includes such beach nesters as the Willet, Piping Plover, and Least Tern.

Offshore islands: Although Connecticut has only small offshore islands, their insular nature sets them apart from inland habitats. They exist in several types: areas of exposed bedrock, deposits of glacial till, and sand deposited by coastal currents. The latter islands may change rapidly over time. For example, sand spits can become sandy islands after a storm, whereas existing sandy islands continually change their shape. Offshore islands support coastal woodland, scrub, and beach plant communities. All are most notable as breeding areas for birds, because they are less subject to mammalian predators than mainland environments. Sandy areas serve as breeding sites for species like the Least Tern and Piping Plover, whereas the Common and Roseate Tern may inhabit offshore rocks. Islands with coastal woodland and scrub are used by a variety of heron and egret species for nesting.

Successional habitats: All of the habitats above exist not only in space but in time. As written, their descriptions assume that they have reached an approximately steady state. In reality, all habitats are dynamic. Storms, disease, drought and a host of other conditions continually shape them. Certain earlier stages in habitat development are particularly notable or widespread, so are considered separately under this heading. These include:

Old fields: Ecologists refer to habitats going through a generally predictable series of changes after disturbance as undergoing secondary succession. Abandoned agricultural land, clear cut land or otherwise disturbed areas tend to go through such changes as they revert to forest. They are aptly termed old fields. Some, like earlier stages of Pitch Pine sand plains, may reforest slowly because they develop in poor, sandy soils. A number of animal species are adapted to inhabit these successional environments.

Grasslands and herbaceous habitats: after certain types of disturbance, notably repeated fires in locations with poor, sandy soil, sites may develop into grasslands vegetated by particularly the native grass Little Bluestem. However, without continued disturbance these areas eventually succeed to woody vegetation. Another grassland type becoming more frequent with us is the beaver meadow. After beavers vacate an area, the ponds they create drain and grasses and sedges come to dominate the wet soil for a time. A third type of herbaceous habitat develops adjacent to marshes if the slope of the land is gentle. In these cases habitats dominated by Switchgrass, Reed Canary Grass, sedges or Sensitive Fern may develop, although these and beaver meadows would appear to be better termed marshes themselves.

Rocky summits: The physical environment of the summit of many hills is rather distinctive in that it is more exposed, generally very dry and nutrient poor (rain drains away from the summit and carries nutrients with it) and has little if any soil. Such locations may exhibit characteristics of primary succession: initial colonization of the physical environment (especially large boulders) by living organisms. Lichens and mosses are important elements of such habitats, as is Deschampsia grass and tree and shrub species adapted to colonizing early successional environments. Many of today's rocky summits owe their appearance not only to the summit environment, but also to 18th and 19th century events like logging, forest fires and agriculture, which resulted in the soils of these locations eroding away. Even so, prevailing summit conditions may arrest succession at an early stage or permit it to occur only very slowly.

Traprock ridges: Traprock, known to geologists as basalt, erodes slowly compared with the surrounding sedimentary rock, so today exists as a series of north-south ridges in central Connecticut. These ridges are the remains of ancient lava flows. Plants less common in acid soils like Ebony Spleenwort are found on comparatively neutral traprock soils. The rock slides (talus slopes) typical of these ridges provide good habitat for snakes, including the Northern Copperhead. The talus slopes provide several distinct microenvironments as a consequence of the physics of air movement through the rocks.

Calcareous habitats: Most of Connecticut's soils are acidic in nature, but soils derived from calcium-bearing minerals are only weakly acidic to basic. These areas are the remains of extremely ancient coral reefs. Although from a wildlife perspective such habitats are not necessarily very different from those of structurally similar acid habitats (although their insect fauna may be quite different), a variety of plant species are characteristic of calcareous soils. As the habitats are moderately extensive and distinctive features of the Connecticut landscape, considering them separately seems warranted.

Uplands: Calcareous uplands can have quite distinctive

herbaceous floras, including limestone-loving ferns like Maidenhair Spleenwort and Walking Fern.

Swamps: Calcareous swamps are distinguished from acidic ones in their distinctive flora. Species like Yellow Lady's Slipper are characteristic.

Fens: Although similar in some respects to bogs, fens are not highly acidic environments. As such, they have a distinctive flora that is associated with low acid conditions.

WHAT MAKES A SPECIES ENDANGERED?

I now return to the question posed earlier: which species are properly called endangered? Especially at the local level, the terms rare and endangered are not necessarily synonyms. Within Connecticut, is a species endangered if its rarity is the consequence of being near its range limit? Well, in some instances yes, and in some no.

Initial considerations: Endangered, quite simply, means to be in danger. In the case of species, the danger is of becoming extinct. Regional governments have expanded this definition to include species in danger of becoming locally extinct, or more precisely locally extirpated. However, this expanded definition can lead to logical difficulties. Because we are concerned here with endangered species issues in Connecticut, let's consider local endangerment further.

I begin by examining the case of migratory birds. Because birds can fly, they are

Eastern Spadefoot

great colonizers and dispersers. Their dispersal ability allows excess individuals from prime areas to spill over into less suitable regions. However, when they do so they usually have lower reproductive success. The existence of such "sink" habitats (you might say, places where birds with nowhere else to live go down the drain) have been known to ecologists for decades. If we extrapolate this situation to birds occupying marginal habitats at their range periphery, local populations are likely to be tied more closely to conditions at the heart of their range than to local conditions.

Not surprisingly, as my own work on Connecticut forest birds has repeatedly shown, populations tend to be lower or even rare at range limits. These populations are in many cases likely to be sustained only by continued immigration from elsewhere. Would it really be correct to call such fringe populations endangered? The issues are actually more complex than this, but the point here is that defining a species as endangered requires a much broader perspective than simply considering local population status.

Now consider the rather different situation of species with poor dispersal ability. In the case of Connecticut's only lizard, the Northern Five-lined Skink, tiny populations have survived in isolated pockets for millennia. How have such small populations managed to persist to the present? Have these northernmost populations begun showing adaptive alterations in their behavior, anatomy, or physiology, or are there some ultimate limits beyond which lizards are incapable of surpassing? In this case, local management action may have meaningful conservation impact, although even in this situation arguments can be made that such species are not of the highest conservation importance.

So in short, in the endangered species arena the closer one looks at the issues the more complex they become. Similar statements could be made about every branch of science. We may paraphrase the Heisenberg Uncertainty Principle from physics to read, "the more something is studied, the less it appears that we know about it." Such a view applies here, and as with the nature of particles considered by Heisenberg, only a more general theory will lead us to greater understanding.

A new view: "Good philosophers soar alone like eagles, and not in flocks like starlings," Galileo is reported to have said. Indeed, for there to be science, scientists must be philosophers, and good philosophers must have the capacity to think independently. Otherwise, how would there ever be new ideas? Galileo's "new," correct, but decidedly unpopular idea was that the Sun was the center of the solar system. He argued this case based on his direct observational evidence of how the solar system operated.

Of course, the second century BC Greek mathematician Aristarchus had long since deduced much the same about the relationship of the Earth to the Sun, by applying the philosophical logic of geometry and trigonometry to direct measurements he could make. He lived in a world where independence of spirit was a virtue, and where holding up dogma to the rigors of logic and experimentation was valued. But that world, the world of empirical science, fell from favor for nearly two millennia. Only determined spirits like Galileo revived the tradition.

As in Galileo's day, established dogma continues to cloud thinking so that observational evidence is not seen clearly. In the world of locally endangered species, for example, a tradition exists whereby endangered rank is conferred principally based on a species' status within the arbitrary boundaries of states. This tradition has clouded the picture of conservation by inadequately considering the wider view of a species' status throughout its entire range.

I have been aware since my first days in the endangered species arena that there were major unresolved issues concerning how locally endangered species are designated. Since those early days I have thought through many of those topics, and have developed a new philosophy of regional endangered species conservation. In order to characterize my evolving view, I begin with a hypothetical situation that I posed to a colleague. Although not quite in the Galilean style of a dialogue, the intent is much the same:

"The Saltmarsh Sharp-tailed Sparrow is a common inhabitant of salt marshes along the coast, although it has suffered declines at some locations. Along the Connecticut River, it is abundant at the river mouth in the towns of Old Lyme and Old Saybrook, but as one travels upriver it quickly drops out as its salt marsh habitat disappears. Just upriver from Old Lyme in Lyme, the Saltmarsh Sharp-tailed Sparrow is rare, and occurs at only a few locations. One spot at which it occurs is not even a salt marsh, but a sedge meadow that is kept from growing up to shrubs by annual mowing. Should we then consider the Saltmarsh Sharp-tailed Sparrow endangered in Lyme? Suppose you are a member of the Lyme Conservation Commission, and have the resources to accomplish two of three conservation priorities in town- 1) purchasing a parcel of mature forest that will connect two existing areas of state forest, keeping the area as contiguous forest, 2) purchasing a privately held piece of the extensive cattail marshes at Lord Cove, thereby furthering the complete protection of this system, and 3) purchasing the sedge meadow in which the rare Saltmarsh Sharp-tailed Sparrow occurs, and arranging additional expenditures each year to keep the parcel from growing up to shrubs. Into which baskets would you place your conservation eggs? How would you prioritize these three options?"

Let's consider a present example of a local endangered

Sharp-tailed sparrow

issue: the Upland Sandpiper, which is listed as State Endangered in New Hampshire, Connecticut, Massachusetts and Rhode Island, but which I think is better termed peripherally-occurring in these regions and not of great local conservation concern. In the Northeast this prairie species is associated with man-made habitats. Its eastern populations have indeed declined as forest and suburbanization has reclaimed agricultural land, but it has a vast continental distribution centered in the plains and agricultural provinces of the continent. Continental population surveys have shown not a decline, but a significant long-term increase.

With respect to natural habitat distributions, the persistence of the Upland Sandpiper in the Northeast may be better considered a testament to its adaptability than as a conservation concern. Notably, those grassland species still persisting in the Northeast are often those with wide continental distributions and large populations. Grassland bird species in general inhabit an inherently variable environment, and appear to have evolved mechanisms for responding to such variation, including undergoing considerable annual change in distribution and abundance, and being able to locate habitat opportunistically.

Efforts have been directed in Connecticut toward creating artificial prairies for species like the Upland Sandpiper. However, we might question whether creation of grasslands in an urbanized Northeastern state is a prudent expenditure of conservation capital. Examine, for example, what happens when we reverse the situation. Suppose the conservation agencies of South Dakota decided to declare the Tufted Titmouse endangered, because it occurs in only a handful of planted woodlands in the eastern corner of the state. How would we in the Northeast, where the species is common and expanding its range, view an attempt by South Dakota to enhance Tufted Titmouse numbers by planting, irrigating and perpetually managing more extensive forest stands? Would we view this as a prudent expenditure of conservation funds, or would it seem more valuable for South Dakota to invest its efforts into restoring native prairie, thereby making these sites again suitable for the state's indigenous prairie wildlife? So, should we acquire and perpetually manipulate on behalf of prairie birds a 100 acres grassland island in otherwise forested, expensive Connecticut, or acquire 1,000 acres of low maintenance grassland in prairie, inexpensive South Dakota?

A key practical criterion for making regional conservation decisions is what habitats are possible given present climatic, physical, and biotic conditions, and prevailing patterns of human land use. Within this context, a continental view is essential for examining ecological systems and formulating an effective approach toward developing endangered species policy. Species occurrence within a state boundary alone is an insufficient criterion.

To this should be added: 1) the geographic region of principal natural habitat distribution, 2) continental distribution, 3) long term continent-wide population trends, 4) historic distributions in light of natural and anthropogenic habitats, 5) historic distributions within the context of the extent of ecologically sustainable natural habitat, 6) degree of human perturbation of natural systems, 7) probability of substantively impacting species survival through local management efforts.

Developing a regional conservation policy: Let's add a few more pieces of the puzzle. Based on my own research on the large-scale patterns of distribution of forest birds in Connecticut, the following are clear: 1) even common species are not uniformly distributed across the landscape, 2) the forest bird community is a highly heterogeneous one composed of species with widely divergent habitat requirements, 3) any one tract, even a very large one, does not contain the entire complement of species present in the forest community, much less the probability of having self-sustaining populations of all the species.

If we put these observations together, we get a picture of a forest ecosystem in Connecticut that we have not even begun to protect adequately. We need a series of very large tracts situated throughout the state if we are to preserve this community. This is especially true considering that remaining forest tracts are becoming increasingly fragmented. Consider, for example, that although forest is the principal natural habitat of the state, it is disappearing at the rate of 6,000 acres/year! Research has shown repeatedly that fragmented forests are far inferior in providing suitable habitat for birds and other forest ecosystem members.

I propose that in our conservation efforts we need to engage in what we might call ecological triage. We must consider what the prevailing ecological conditions in our region are, and what habitats we have a realistic chance of adequately protecting. We cannot afford to dissipate efforts into areas where we can have little real impact. Considering the pace of habitat destruction and our finite conservation resources, we have to make wise choices. The issue is not preserving everything, but preserving something. The logical choice would be to work particularly toward protecting our principal regional ecological systems like forest. From the standpoint of protecting biological diversity, this strategy makes the most sense as well, as forests are among the most diverse of our natural habitats.

Oak-Dominated Forest 6

There is a famous chorus in Giuseppe Verdi's opera *Nabucco* that begins "Fly my heart on golden wings." Such could be the anthem of Connecticut's prevailing forest habitat: oak-dominated forest. To say that it's heart flew north to establish itself in our region would not be a great overstatement, although its development did not quite occur overnight.

By 17,000 years ago, the landscape of southern New England had only begun to emerge from millennia beneath ice. Arctic tundra conditions prevailed until 14,000 years ago, when boreal conifer forests began to colonize the thawing landscape. These forests were replaced in turn by conifer-northern hardwood forests beginning about 10,000 years ago. It was at this time that oaks first began to make their appearance. By 6,000 years ago, pollen records show that oaks were 40 percent of the forest, or roughly similar to conditions at present.

But how did those trees get here, and why did some arrive and others not? Species like the cottonwoods could be carried north on the wind by virtue of their tiny seeds and peculiar "flotation" devices. Cottonwoods are, in fact, named for the cottony structures that surround their seeds. Their travel can be understood by thinking of what happens when a rock and piece of paper are dropped simultaneously. When the rock falls, it continually accelerates down due to the action of gravity. The paper accelerates briefly, but then floats slowly down at a constant speed, its "terminal velocity." This occurs because the downward acceleration of the paper is countered by an upward force exerted by air on the paper. The phenomenon is known as air resistance, and is most effective at slowing the fall of objects that are light and have large surface areas. Cottonwood seeds with their surrounding cottony structures satisfy both these criteria. When another force is added, like the force provided by wind, not only is the descent of the seed slowed, but the seed can be carried by the wind horizontally. Cottonwood seeds can travel for miles, and thereby distribute themselves rapidly.

Other species like elms produce tiny seeds surrounded by flat wings. The seeds can float on the wind, but they float as well like miniature rafts on water. Both our local elm species are associated with riverbanks. They set seeds in early spring when rivers are typically experiencing spring floods, so seeds can be carried long distances from the parent tree. In addition to the elms, trees like maples, birches and hornbeam also have winged seeds that assist with dispersal.

But what about the most common of our trees: the oaks? They have large, heavy seeds that are not transported by wind. To understand how they colonized the emerging landscapes of post-glacial times, we must turn to the lowly Blue Jay. The hardy, adaptable, belligerent and acorn-loving Blue jay is virtually ignored by birdwatchers. It is common everywhere, it harasses other birds, it preys upon nestlings, and so has been afforded a status among bird aficionados only marginally higher than that of the park pigeon.   However, it is a native species, and by virtue of its success and abundance we may reasonably postulate that its collectively mighty wings played a major role in carrying north oaks to southern New England.

To be sure, the Blue Jay had help in this task. The forest also scurried north on the feet of another lowly but immensely successful native, the Gray Squirrel. Both these species hoard acorns and are particularly important dispersers of seeds, because many of the seeds they cache are not retrieved. The remainder is left to germinate. Individual Blue Jays routinely cache 3,000-5000 acorns each fall.

Unlike the Gray Squirrel, the Blue Jay also travels over great distances, and these movements likely aided further the transport of acorns north. The extent to which the Blue Jay is migratory is often overlooked, as members of its species are with us year round. However, it is highly migratory. It leaves Connecticut in droves every fall, and flock after flock can be seen returning in spring. In fact, its abundance over much of the state averages far lower in winter than in summer, and remaining birds tend to accumulate near the coast where climatic conditions are moderated by the influence of Long Island Sound. When I mapped the distribution of forest-dwelling Blue Jays in the region, the highest summer densities were in northeast Connecticut, whereas the highest winter densities were along the coast.

Summer densities of the Blue Jay were greatest in northeast Connecticut. Light areas indicate low density, gray areas mid-range density, dark areas high density.

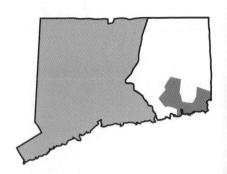

Winter densities of the Blue Jay were greatest in southeast Connecticut. Light areas indicate low density, gray areas mid-range density, dark areas high density.

And what of plants that bear fleshy fruits? Here again, birds can be important dispersers. Some of our common tree, shrub and vine species like cherries, hollies, viburnums, dogwoods, elderberries, briars, blackberries and even Poison Ivy produce fleshy fruits. Birds like the American Robin, Cedar Waxwing and Gray Catbird all feed upon fruits when they are available. Many of these fruits have hard, indigestible seeds, so their fleshy part acts as an inducement for birds to eat the fruits and carry seeds in their stomachs to some new location, where they deposit them as waste.

In short, animals of a number of types, but particularly birds because of their mobility, are important dispersers of native plants. They are likely to have played a major role in the establishment of our present forest community. Such phenomena are not restricted to the Northeast, but are common in many communities.

One discovery I made on remote tropical islands was that even a single animal species can exert a profound influence on the course of forest development. In that case, the key disperser of large seeds was not a bird but another winged animal, a fruit-eating bat. On islands with fruit bats, large-seeded tree species were common in disturbed areas reverting to forest. On islands where the fruit bats had been hunted to extinction, areas reverting to native forest had seedlings of small-fruited species that were eaten by small birds, but large seeded species were virtually absent. Clearly, the wings of bats, like the wings of birds, provided an effective means of dispersal for large seeded trees.

Despite the various modes of tree dispersal into Connecticut, the forests of our region remain conspicuously limited in their variety of species. Any forest tract is likely to be dominated by only a handful of species. By comparison, similar-looking forests growing in similar climates in the southern Appalachian Mountains are comparatively diverse. They are notable especially in their greater number of flowering trees, like silverbells and buckeyes. Some flowering species in the Appalachians that are absent in southern New England, like Eastern Redbud, are unable to survive our winters. Others like the Black Locust survive and reproduce readily here, although they never colonized the area on their own. During glacial times, the deciduous forest survived in isolated pockets across the Southeast. As climates warmed and these founder pockets expanded and reconnected, some species had the capacity to expand northward, but others did not. We may, therefore, presume that history has played a major role in determining the composition of our regional forests.

FIELD TRIP
Pumpkin Hill Wildlife Management Area, Chaplin

Directions: Pumpkin Hill may be reached by traveling east on Rt. 6 to the junction of Rt. 198. Follow Rt. 198 north about two miles to the junction of Pumpkin Hill Rd. Go right, and follow the road up a hill. Parking places are present all along this road. To reach a favorite spot, travel past the hilltop to the bottom of a long hill. A wildlife impoundment is situated on the left side of the road, and Pumpkin Hill is behind it.

Equipment: There are many roads and trails through the Pumpkin Hill area that are easy to follow and require no special equipment. However, there are a number of wet areas present, so hiking boots are a good choice for footwear. Ticks are present during much of the year, and black flies and mosquitoes can be ferocious into early summer, so long pants, socks, long sleeve shirts, hats and insect repellent are also wise choices.   Binoculars and field guides are helpful. Pumpkin Hill itself is steep in spots and quite rocky, so if you choose to explore it take special precautions on wet days to avoid slipping on rocks.

The habitat: As with any landscape, Pumpkin Hill is a mosaic of habitats. There are open deciduous swamps, ponds, mixed deciduous upland forest, upland oak-hickory forest, and dry ridge top oak forests. The last two of these are the most widespread, and will be the ones I focus on here.

The characteristic forests on uplands throughout much of the state are forests dominated by oaks. Such forests were once referred to as oak-chestnut forests, but American Chestnut (*Castanea dentata*) has long since been virtually eliminated by blight. Today chestnuts survive only as sprouts and saplings that grow from the roots of trees now long gone. Trunks of their highly rot resistant wood may still be seen lying on the forest floor. Without the fast-growing, formerly massive chestnuts, the oaks are now the key forest species. Black (*Quercus velutina*), Red (*Q. rubra*) and White Oak (*Q. alba*) form the backbone of most regional forests, although another related group, the hickories, also can be quite important. The most typical species on better sites are Pignut (*C. glabra*) and Shagbark Hickory (*C. ovata*).

Both oaks and hickories present identification problems, and the oaks in particular are notorious for hybridizing to produce intermediate forms. Examining fruits (acorns and hickory nuts) generally provides the most reliable way for separating both groups to species, although except for fall this is of little help. During the remainder of the year, typical examples of Black Oak may be separated from those of Red Oak by the generally more blocky bark of the former, and the vertical, smooth stripes on the upper trunks of the latter. In summer, the wider ends and hairier surfaces of Black Oak leaves help to differentiate them from the more symmetrical, hairless leaves of Red Oak. The buds of Black Oak twigs also tend toward being whitish hairy, whereas those of Red Oak tend to be shiny red-brown. White Oak is easy to identify year-round because of its whitish-gray, scaly bark.

These oaks actually form two natural groups, with white oak relatives exhibiting rounded leaf lobes that contrast with the pointed leaf tips of red oak relatives. White oaks also have acorns that germinate in fall, whereas red oak acorns germinate only after going through a winter season (called winter scarifying of the acorns). Both groups have high levels of tannic acid in their acorns, which makes them unpalatable to people. However, the white oaks are less strongly acidic, and native people soaked them in streams to remove the water-soluble tannic acid. Once they removed the acid, they pounded the acorns into flour and consumed them.

The oaks as a group include some of our longest-lived and largest species of forest trees. Specimens of Black and White Oak I have examined in virgin stands have been over 100 ft tall, 48 inches in diameter (measurements of diameter are traditionally taken at breast height, and diameter measurements are abbreviated dbh for diameter at breast height), and nearly 300 years old (although white oaks to 600 years in age have been recorded). Remarkably, I have found individual oaks of these proportions scattered through a number of forests in Connecticut. One magnificent Red Oak I found in remote Killingly woodland had a dbh of 40 inches. A Black Oak I found at Pumpkin Hill had a dbh of 34 inches. Although Connecticut forests do not exhibit extensive virgin conditions anywhere in the state, patches of such enormous trees are now present with increasing frequency as our regional forests mature.

The hickories also present some identification problems, particularly the Red (*C. ovalis*) and Pignut Hickory. All species of hickories have compound leaves, meaning that a leaf is composed of separate leaflets joined together by a stem-like structure called a rachis. The Red Hickory tends to have leaves composed more frequently of seven leaflets, whereas the Pignut more frequently has five leaflets. However, they are best identified from their nuts. It appears to me that the Red Hickory is more frequent in northern Connecticut and the Pignut more frequent in the southern half of the state, but the species are so problematic in their identity that it is hard for me to be sure. Authorities, in fact, differ as to the validity of these species, and most today lump them into one species, so attempting to differentiate them may not be that important.

Red oak

The Shagbark Hickory, in contrast to these two, is an easily identified and particularly handsome tree. Even young specimens show the characteristic sheets of peeling bark that give mature specimens a grandly ragged appearance. Shagbark Hickory is more prevalent at richer sites, whereas the other two species are often found on poorer soils. Shagbark Hickory like the oaks is a long-lived species, and virgin specimens have attained ages of 300 years and diameters of 48 inches. In the Pumpkin Hill area, I have found some fine stands of mature hickories, which in spots even outnumber the oaks. One Red Hickory measured 24 inches dbh.

Although oaks and hickories form the backbone of many of our regional forests, other species are also important members of the forest community. Red Maple is one of the most indomitable species found in any forest. It is the quintessential ecological generalist. It may be found in every habitat from open swamp to bone dry ridge top, and its range extends from the boreal forests of Newfoundland, where it co-occurs with spruce and fir, to the Everglades of Florida, where it co-occurs with baldcypress and mahogany. At Pumpkin Hill, Red Maple is found on the dry, rocky summit of the hill itself, on moist slopes, along streams, and in swamps.

An additional oak-dominated community is present at the summit of Pumpkin Hill. The shallow, rocky soils and tendency of water to drain away from hilltops make conditions there particularly poor. In these poor conditions, forests are dominated by Chestnut Oak (*Q. prinus*) and Scarlet Oak (*Q. coccinea*), along with the understory shrubs Huckleberry (*Gaylussacia baccata*), Lowbush Blueberry (*Vaccinium angustifolium*) and Round-leaved Blueberry (*V. vacillans*). Chestnut Oak is in the white oak group, and has leaves with numerous lobes. Scarlet Oak is such a handsome and tolerant member of the red oak group that it has been brought into cultivation. Its leaves are so deeply dissected that they appear lacy. They turn deep scarlet in late autumn, and it is for this trait that the species is named.

Wildlife: There are fewer kinds of reptiles and amphibians in upland oak forests than in moister situations. However, a number of kinds are still present. In fact, one of the most abundant of all vertebrates (animals with backbones) occurs in these forests. Even in dry oak woods, the ubiquitous Red-backed Salamander may be found under leaf litter, under rocks and under fallen logs. I have also found the Slimy Salamander in moister oak forests adjacent to hemlock ravines, although it is known only from extreme western Connecticut.

Several frogs and toads inhabit the oak forest. The Wood Frog may be found in leaf litter, and is particularly conspicuous on rainy nights even in mid-summer when the frogs are actively moving. Two species of tree-dwelling frogs, the Spring Peeper and Gray

Tree frog, also occur in these forests. The American Toad is the most widespread woodland toad in our region, and is typical of especially those regions underlain by crystalline rocks like schist. The Fowler's Toad, in contrast, is typical of sandy soils such as those deposited by glacial activity. A significant deposit from glacial melt water occurs along the Natchaug River where it flows through Chaplin, so I have found Fowler's Toads near the Pumpkin Hill area.

Gray Tree Frog

Scattered through our most common forest habitats are low spots that collect with water each spring and then dry out over the summer. These areas, termed vernal (temporary) pools, are among the most important breeding habitats for a number of spring breeding amphibians. Because they are generally unconnected to more permanent bodies of water, they lack some of the predators like fish that occur in permanent water. This reduction in predators improves the probability of survival by amphibian eggs and larvae (juvenile hatchling stages). The Spotted Salamander, Wood Frog, Spring Peeper, Gray Tree Frog, American Toad and Fowler's Toad all breed in these pools. Another species, the Blue spotted Salamander, also occurs in some towns in Northeast Connecticut. I have found this species inhabiting wet areas on glacial sands like those in Chaplin, so they should be searched for in the Pumpkin Hill area.

The oak-dominated forest is one of the region's principal population reservoirs for many forest bird species. Data I gathered on habitat use by forest birds demonstrated that species like the

Eastern Wood Pewee, Red-eyed Vireo, Wood Thrush, Worm-eating Warbler and Rose-breasted Grosbeak were closely associated with oak-dominated forest. Moreover, permanent resident species like the Red-bellied Woodpecker moved disproportionately into this habitat for the winter. Other species, including forest birds with more generalized habitat requirements, were present in oak forests in approximately the proportions at which this habitat is present. Species like the Downy Woodpecker, Great Crested Flycatcher, Black-capped Chickadee, White-breasted Nuthatch, Black-and-white Warbler, Ovenbird and Scarlet Tanager fell into this category.

In addition to these characteristic oak forest species, several other species with more limited distributions are found in this habitat, and occur at Pumpkin Hill. I first found the Cerulean Warbler nesting at Pumpkin Hill in 1978. Since that time it has firmly established itself as a breeder. Other local breeding sites have been occupied and vacated, but the Pumpkin Hill population has been present consistently. The species is associated with mature deciduous forest, and these forests are widespread in the area. Even selective logging operations carried out on the property have not eliminated birds, and I have been suspicious that partial opening of the canopy in the presence of remaining large trees may even be beneficial for the species. On the other hand, the distribution of nesters there has shifted over the years, so the influence of logging operations on populations warrants further investigation.

Another species near its northern range limit at Pumpkin Hill is the Hooded Warbler. Like the Cerulean Warbler, its occurrence has been consistent. In this case, the dense understory that has grown up following selective logging appears to have benefited this shrub-dwelling species. Still another southerly-distributed species at Pumpkin Hill that appears to benefit from selective logging is the Whip-poor-will. As recently as 2001, I found a nesting bird next to an area recently logged.

One other southern species that has made appearances at

Pumpkin Hill is the Kentucky Warbler. This bird is virtually absent from Connecticut during the breeding season, although occasionally birds "overshoot" their normal breeding range while migrating north in spring. I have presumed that the occasional appearance of the Kentucky Warbler at Pumpkin Hill may be related to the consistent occurrence of other southerly-distributed birds there.

The mammals of the Pumpkin Hill area include a number of predatory species. The Red (preferring more open areas) and Gray Fox (preferring wooded areas) are both present, and their larger cousin the Coyote is also present. These canine relatives sometimes associate with domestic dogs and other animals. On one early morning on Pumpkin Hill Road I watched several neighborhood dogs sitting in the middle of the road with a Red Fox. All appeared to be getting on fine. In this same area I also observed a family of Groundhogs sharing the same burrow system with a Red Fox, also in apparent harmony. I had read that both these burrowing animals did so on occasion, but actually seeing it was something else.

Still another predator that appears well established at Pumpkin Hill and adjacent Natchaug State Forest is the Bobcat. Winter expeditions to Pumpkin Hill reveal numerous bobcat tracks (like large house cat tracks) in fresh snow. The species' characteristic bloodcurdling shrieks also may be heard on nighttime expeditions to the area. Actually seeing this primarily nocturnal and secretive animal is quite a feat, however. In the past few decades I have only seen Bobcats two or three times, even though they are not particularly rare.

More easily detected mammals include the usual daytime contingent of forest mammals like the Gray Squirrel and Eastern Chipmunk. Another species present, the Southern Flying Squirrel, is a common nocturnal mammal that may be detected by its characteristic but nearly ultrasonic squeaks. Once its voice is learned, a nighttime trip to the forest reveals just how common it is.

The wetland complexes that dissect Pumpkin Hill attract their own characteristic species of mammals. I have seen the Beaver, Muskrat and River Otter in the vicinity.

Closing thoughts: There are an infinite number of oak forests to explore in Connecticut. One near Pumpkin Hill, Natchaug State Forest (extending through Pomfret, Eastford, Chaplin and Hampton), is one of the largest state forests in Connecticut. Other good places to see oak-dominated forest are Nehantic State Forest in Lyme and East Lyme, Meshomasic State Forest in East Hampton, Portland and Glastonbury, Nathan Hale State Forest in Coventry, Cockaponset State Forest in Haddam and Chester, Sleeping Giant State Park in Hamden, and Paugussett State Forest in Newtown.

Mixed Deciduous Forest

Peculiarly enough, the crest of my barn roof has proven to be a good place for contemplation. I have spent a good deal of time replacing shingles there during the past year, so it has become a place I know well. From my perch I can consider two quite different versions of the natural world, as the barn sits on the dividing line between them. I find satisfaction in my ability to read the two landscapes, and understand at least some of what they have to teach. Although my investigations of natural landscapes have not provided me with every answer I might wish, the focus on them has proven for me to be a substantive one. Finding such a focus has, in fact, been a principal goal of mine for much of my life.

I have been haunted since my college days by the specter of Ivan Illych, a character in a Russian short story. Ivan Illych was a petty bureaucrat, whose life became a mad obsession of acquiring possessions and status, until one day while adjusting parlor drapes he fell. The injuries he sustained resulted in his progressive decline toward death, although as he did so his family hardly noticed amidst the bustle of their shallow existence. It was only during his solitary decline that he realized what in life had true value.

During my first employment after college, the Illych-like nature of my position so appalled me that I endured it for little more than a year before I resigned. Even the lifetime security of the government womb was insufficient enticement for me to remain. I feared too much looking back, like Ivan Illych, on a pointless existence, for which security was poor consolation. I was in subsequent years offered opportunities for similar employment, which I reflexively turned down, and chose instead to follow a rather more difficult but acceptable path.

Considering those decisions, it is with some irony that I now find myself living in the grandest home, with the most elegantly appointed parlors, and with elements of that status which I have considered so irrelevant. So it is not surprising to me that as I climb to the roofs of our barns to begin the next round of maintenance on each, I find I am still not free of Ivan Illych. The possibility of senseless

Red Trillium

injury leads me to contemplate how I have spent my life. I have thought that I had some notion of life's true values, and as I perform the menial tasks of maintenance, I labor also to determine whether I have spent sufficient time pursuing those values.

The fact that I can decipher something of the landscapes below me suggests to me that I have achieved some measure of success in reaching this goal. Like Illych, I have discovered that those aspects of life which are transcendent are found most readily within the natural world. To understand facets of this world is to uncover the most basic of truths. Let us examine that roof view, and discover some of the truths that may be gleaned from it:

To the east, the barn looks out on a ridge top of dry, poor soil left by glacial activity 17,000 years earlier. This history dictates that the land should be vegetated by pines and oaks, which it indeed is. Eastern White Pine, which is tolerant of dry and poor conditions, joins with other dry site specialists like Scarlet Oak, Chestnut Oak and Huckleberry to populate this landscape.

To the west, the soil shifts abruptly to a different type, the consequence in part of geological processes that bring water close to the surface. The remains of decaying plants have collected here, and in the presence of abundant moisture have developed into black and rich soil. Because of its fertility, the area was kept in farmland well into the 20th century, unlike the adjacent woodlands on poorer soil, which were last farmed in the mid-19th century. On rich soil, the former farmland is regenerating to an entirely different type of forest that is composed of tree species requiring these conditions. Several mature trees once at the borders of fields have provided seed sources. Species like White Ash, Shagbark Hickory, Yellow Poplar, American Elm and the usually uncommon Butternut have produced abundant saplings in former fields. In areas that have been abandoned longer, these saplings have matured, and the forest has diversified into a community characteristic of rich and moist sites. These forests may be referred to as mixed deciduous forests.

So what is to be learned from this view? Proximately, we may observe that the physical environment and its history exert profound influences over the biotic environment. But ultimately, we may come to understand something more. Upon careful reflection, one can conclude that this and every natural landscape produce something that might most precisely be referred to as music. The instruments are the living components, the trees, the flowers, the birds, and in concert they perform the present movement of a first symphony. The timbre and color of the performance is indeed shaped by elements that predate life, so it is a synthesis of living and non-living: a first grand synthesis. It is the place from which springs art; its underlying basis is the birth of beauty.

If we were alien beings examining Earth wheeling through space, we would be confronted in this void by the planet that produces music. The universe itself is said to sing at 57 octaves below human hearing, with a frequency so low that we do not live long enough to experience the passage of two successive waves. But our planet produces music by and for the living. One cosmologist has said that if we could understand the workings of the universe we would know the mind of God. By simply being aware of our surroundings, perhaps we can already hear his voice.

FIELD TRIP
Bartlett Brook Wildlife Management Area, Lebanon

Directions: Take Rt. 16 in Lebanon north to Goshen Hill Rd. Turn right and drive about 0.7 miles to the sign for Bartlett Brook. Turn right and follow the road in to a parking area. The dirt road that leads from the parking lot can be used to explore the area.

Equipment: Hiking boots or rubber boots are strongly recommended for exploring the area, which is rather wet over much of its extent. Ticks are present from spring to fall, and black flies and mosquitoes can be ferocious into early summer, so long pants, socks, long sleeve shirts, hats and insect repellent are also wise choices. Binoculars and field guides are helpful. The trails can be muddy, so take precautions to avoid slipping.

The habitat: Bartlett Brook is a maze of swamps and uplands, with much of the upland vegetated by moist forest. One could describe the moist forest as a transition environment between permanently wet swamps and persistently drier uplands. In short, this forest is part of a continuum from wet to dry, but an extensive enough component of it to have developed a character of its own. Because moist forest is a rather intermediate sort of habitat, species more typical of the swamp and drier forest make an appearance in it, but other species are characteristic principally of it. The combination of such elements is in part responsible for the higher diversity of the moist forest, which may be spoken of as the mixed deciduous forest.

One of the key species of this environment is the Yellow Poplar (*Liriodendron tulipifera*), one of the monarchs of the New England forest. It is actually not a poplar at all but a relative of the magnolias. For this reason, its alternate name, Tulip Tree, is perhaps more appropriate, as it reflects the singularly unique tulip shape of its leaves and the spectacular orange and green blossoms it produces in late spring. The Tulip Tree is one of the region's fastest growing. On good soil it can attain a height of 120 feet in 50 years, and old growth specimens have been reported to heights of 198 feet, diameters of 12 feet and ages of 300 years. Its comparatively

Yellow Poplar

fast growth is often obvious when one compares the size of similarly aged oaks and Tulip Trees growing in the same forest stand. The Tulips can dwarf the other trees.

Another hallmark tree of moist forest is the White Ash (*Fraxinus americana*). Like the Tulip Tree, it grows fast and attains considerable size. Mature specimens to 125 feet and 7 feet in diameter have been reported. White Ash has compound leaves, meaning that its leaves are composed of series of smaller elements, leaflets, which are connected together by means of a stem-like rachis. The furrowed gray bark and thick, straight branches of the White Ash make it easily identified in summer and winter. The stout forms of bare winter trees have been used as symbols of strength.

The Shagbark Hickory (*Carya ovata*) also occurs in moist, rich soil and has compound leaves somewhat like those of the White Ash. However, Shagbark Hickory leaves are arranged alternately on its twigs, whereas White Ash leaves arise directly opposite each other. Mature Shagbark Hickories also exhibit, as their name suggests, sheets of curling, shaggy bark along the length of their trunks. Old specimens are among the most picturesque of our forest trees.

Although now largely gone as a mature canopy tree, the vase-shaped American Elm (*Ulmus americana*) is still fairly common as a medium-sized tree in moister forests. Old specimens have been greatly reduced in numbers by Dutch elm disease, a fungus parasite carried to trees by the Elm Bark Beetle. However, young, fast growing specimens can survive to reproduce and occasionally reach the forest canopy. American Elm is most typical of floodplain forests and swamps, but actually makes superior growth in the better drained soil of moist forests. Similarly, Red Maple (*Acer rubrum*) is most abundant in swamps, but also moves into moist forests. Its relative, Sugar Maple (*A. saccharum*), is more restricted to moist forest environments, as are the comparatively uncommon

Butternut (*Juglans cinerea*) and American Linden (*Tilia americana*).

Of those oaks present in our area, the one most typical of moister forests is the Northern Red Oak (*Quercus rubra*). An oak relative, American Beech (*Fagus grandifolia*), is typical of richer and moister sites, although it is not restricted to them. Together with Sugar Maple and Yellow Birch (*Betula lutea*), the beech forms a typical forest association of the Northeast: beech-birch-maple. Yellow Birch is also a common tree of area swamps.

The moister soils of the mixed deciduous forest give rise not only to an often diverse forest canopy, but also to a diverse understory. Shrubs and understory trees commonly present include Maple-leafed Viburnum (*Viburnum acerifolium*), Nannyberry (*V. lentago*), Arrowwood (*V. recognitum*), Sweet Pepperbush (*Clethra alnifolia*), Highbush Blueberry (*Vaccinium corymbosum*), Flowering Dogwood (*Cornus florida*), Spicebush (*Lindera benzoin*) and Witch Hazel (*Hamamelis virginiana*).

The herbaceous flora of mixed deciduous forests has a diverse component of spring-flowering species. One of the most interesting, albeit a rather locally occurring one, is the May-apple (*Podophyllum peltatum*). Its species name refers to its peltate leaf, a type where the stem attaches to the center of the leaf rather than to an end. When the plant arises from the ground in spring, the leaf is folded about the stem, giving the emerging plant the appearance of a hand with fingers pressed together. Because May-apple often grows colonially, many may emerge simultaneously, producing a sight that can be unearthly.

Other often colonial spring flowering herbs are the Trout Lily (*Erythronium americanum*), Wild Ginger (*Asarum canadense*), Dutchman's Breeches (*Dicentra cucullaria*) and Bloodroot (*Sanguinaria canadensis*). In addition, four species of trilliums, the Red (*Trillium erectum*), White (*T. grandiflorum*), Painted (*T. undulatum*) and Nodding (*T. cernuum*) trilliums may be found in our area, although some are of rather local occurrence. All these are such attractive plants that they have been brought into the garden.

Still other spring flowering natives of richer, moister soil include the Wood Anemone (*Anemone quinquefolia*), Wild Lily-of-the-valley (*Maianthemum canadense*), Solomon's Seal (*Polygonatum biflorum*), False Solomon's Seal (*Smilicina racemosa*), Blue Cohosh (*Caulophyllum thalictroides*), Red Baneberry (*Actea rubra*), White Baneberry (*A. pachypoda*), Jack-in-the-Pulpit (*Arisaema atrorubens*), Ginseng (*Panax quinquefolius*)

Bloodroot

and Dwarf Ginseng (*P. trifolium*). Characteristic ferns include Maidenhair Fern (*Adiantum pedatum*), Lady Fern (*Athyrium filix-femina*), Silvery Spleenwort (*A. thelypteroides*) Broad Beech Fern (*Thelypteris hexagonoptera*), Narrow Beech Fern (*T. phegopteris*) and Marginal Shield Fern (*Dryopteris marginalis*).

Wildlife: Moister habitats favor amphibians, and species like the Red-backed Salamander and Wood Frog may be found inhabiting the forest floor in these mesic areas. I have also found reptiles like the Wood Turtle in moister forests. Moreover, I have found the Eastern Milk Snake and Northern Ringneck Snake in such habitats, although they do not appear to be restricted to them. In northern Connecticut, moist forests also serve as home to one of the region's less common reptiles, the Northern Redbelly Snake.

Bird life of moist, mixed deciduous forest is in many regards similar to that occurring in drier habitats. However, during my surveys of habitat use by forest birds, I found that some species occupied mixed deciduous forest more than would be expected based on this habitat's occurrence. In eastern Connecticut, I estimated that about 14 percent of the forested landscape is vegetated by mixed deciduous forest. However, the proportion of the populations of the Acadian Flycatcher, Hairy Woodpecker (in winter), Downy Woodpecker (year-round), Yellow-throated Vireo, Carolina Wren, Blue-gray Gnatcatcher, American Robin, Gray Catbird, American Redstart and Baltimore Oriole found in this habitat was considerably more than 14 percent.

The Acadian Flycatcher often occurs along stream borders, so an association with these moister areas is not surprising. The Yellow-throated Vireo, American Redstart, Gray Catbird and Baltimore Oriole often inhabit the more open areas bordering wider streams and rivers, so an association with moister, mixed deciduous forest is also to be expected. The association of woodpeckers with such forests has been reported, although these species are not thought to be associated specifically with watercourses. I observed some positive association between the density of dead trees and the presence of moister forests, so the relationship of woodpeckers (which use such trees for feeding) with such forests may reflect the frequency with which dead trees occur in these habitats.

Mammals of moist, mixed deciduous forests are, like the birds, not terribly different from those of drier forests. The usual small mammal contingent of Short-tailed Shrew, White-footed Mouse, Gray Squirrel, Eastern Chipmunk and Southern Flying Squirrel may be found there, along with larger mammals like the Striped Skunk, Raccoon, Gray Fox and Eastern Cottontail. I have also found the tiny Masked Shrew in these habitats.

In recent years, I have begun seeing the Eastern Coyote with increasing frequency in this and other forest types. Moreover, I have observed the Fisher, another comparatively recent Connecticut colonizer, inhabiting mesic forests in our area. I first saw a

Connecticut individual in north Ashford in 1983, about the time when Fishers were first being reported from our region. It was exploring areas along a stream in forests that ranged from conifer-northern hardwoods to mixed deciduous. I have since seen animals in areas ranging from nearly the Massachusetts border in Union to as far south as Hebron. Most individuals I have found have been present near streams, much like their smaller cousin, the Mink, which is often associated with watercourses.

Closing thoughts: Examples of this habitat may be found in most any woodland in Connecticut. Other extensive areas of mixed deciduous forest are found at the State Fish Hatchery in Plainfield, where there are also attractive areas of floodplain forest, and at Salmon River State Forest in Hebron, Nehantic State Forest in East Lyme, and Assekonk Swamp Wildlife Management Area in North Stonington.

Conifer-Northern Hardwood 8

O n a day in May, 1636, Thomas Hooker journeyed through a steep and rugged valley he referred to as Boston Hollow. He was on his way from the growing Massachusetts Bay colony, passing through what would become Northeast Connecticut, to found a new settlement along the banks of the Connecticut River. The rude wilderness outpost he established would become known as Hartford, named for Hertford, England, the birthplace of his colleague Samuel Stone. In those early days, Hartford was vulnerable to attacks by hostile Pequots, but it was thankfully connected to the outside world by the natural highway of the river.

In the 367 years between its founding and the present, Hartford has sprawled outward, such that its modern tentacles now connect with those of the consolidating Boston to Washington megalopolis. Its colonial past has virtually disappeared beneath concrete and glass boxes, although a tiny cemetery from that time remains. It is the plot where Hooker is buried. The exact location of the grave is no longer clear, but in that rare grassy spot there is still some small connection to an earlier and wilder age.

Boston Hollow, in contrast to Hartford, is still a place Hooker might recognize. It lies today at the edge of one of the region's largest remaining tracts of wilderness. It is hard to be sure precisely what it might have looked like during Hooker's passage, although there are some clues. There is Fredrick Church's 19th century painting of Hooker's approach toward Hartford (which still can be seen at the Wadsworth Athenaeum in Hartford). Painted as it was 200 years after the event, however, it is a romanticized vision of the virgin Connecticut landscape. A better view comes from the writings and photographs of early 20th century plant ecologists, who examined the last vestiges of virgin forest in Connecticut. One substantial

Cintonia

stand survived in Colebrook in an environment much like that where Boston Hollow is situated. Other clues come from my own explorations of old growth, some small patches of which are present in the very vicinity of Boston Hollow.

There are today surviving in the Boston Hollow area Eastern White Pines in excess of 100 feet tall. There are as well towering specimens of Northern Red Oak, Eastern Hemlock, White Ash, Yellow Poplar and American Beech. From these, I envision the forest that Thomas Hooker encountered as a ragged canopy of old growth, punctuated by openings created by the fall of forest giants. I imagine a forest majestic in its proportions, but forbidding in its effect. Even on a winter morning today, the groaning trunks of the remaining few old trees conjure thoughts of wolves and mountain lions lurking in the shadows. I expect also that, in passing through such landscapes, Hooker's journey from Massachusetts to Hartford is captured, if not in detail by Church's image, then certainly in its spirit.

Before I describe the forests of the Boston Hollow area, some clarification of terms is required. Earlier plant ecologists have sometimes divided conifer-containing forests of northern areas more finely than I do here. They refer to conifer-transition hardwood associations as distinct from conifer-northern hardwood associations. Within the larger context of New England, such a distinction is a reasonable one. Forests of the north indeed exhibit great dominance by species like maples, beeches and birches (northern hardwoods), whereas forests of the south contain a greater proportion of certain oaks and birches (transition hardwoods). In our state, the latter is the more prevalent association even across much of northern Connecticut.

I choose not to distinguish between these associations because I do not find them sufficiently distinct in our region to warrant separation. Both groups of hardwoods are of importance in our northern forests. Moreover, as I have described for ecoregions, statistical considerations argue for combining such similar categories in order to facilitate comparative analyses. I have retained the name northern hardwoods for this habitat in part because it follows the precedent established in the famous E. Lucy Braun classification of eastern forests. Moreover, I find that the term more clearly differentiates this association from the oak-dominated communities predominating in southern Connecticut.

As I stated in the introductory chapters of this book, our forest communities exist in reality as a continuum of types. When we categorize, we subjectively subdivide this continuum. Such subdivision is warranted when it provides tools useful for understanding patterns and processes in nature, and I find that this less constrained subdivision is more successful at accomplishing these goals. With this as an introduction, let us now examine the conifer-northern hardwood forest.

Field Trip
Boston Hollow, Ashford

Directions: Boston Hollow may be reached by traveling north on Rt. 89 from its junction with Rt. 44. Take Rt. 89 into Westford Center. Just before the center a stone commemorating Hooker's journey may be seen to the right of the road. Go right at Westford Center down a hill, and where the paved road turns right a dirt road continues straight. This is Boston Hollow Road. This ancient dirt road, underlain by colonial era stones, has several pull-offs where cars can be parked. The best is adjacent to where a blue dot hiking trail (the Nipmuck Trail), crosses the road.

Equipment: Hiking boots are strongly recommended for the hike of about two miles to the summit of Boston Hollow. Ticks are present during much of the year, and black flies and mosquitoes can be ferocious into early summer, so long pants, socks, long sleeve shirts, hats and insect repellent are also wise choices. Binoculars and field guides are helpful. The trails are rather steep in spots and quite rocky. Take special precautions on wet days to avoid slipping on the rocks.

The habitat: Boston Hollow is the southernmost extension of the Taconic Plateau in eastern Connecticut. Its greater relief and elevation result in its having a local climate cooler than in uplands to the south. Consequently, a variety of plant and animal species reach their southern range limit along Boston Hollow Road. Mixed conifer-northern hardwood forest is the prevailing vegetation of the region, but other well-developed forest communities can be observed in the vicinity. We will examine several here.

Traveling up the Nipmuck trail from Boston Hollow Road immediately brings to view a small area of very large trees occurring with enough frequency to resemble old growth conditions. Massive Northern Red Oaks (*Quercus rubra*) occur with Eastern White Pine (*Pinus strobus*) and Eastern Hemlock (*Tsuga canadensis*). Mixed in are Sugar Maple (*Acer saccharum*), Red Maple (*A. rubrum*), American Beech (*Fagus grandiflora*), White Ash (*Fraxinus americana*), White Oak (*Q. alba*), Shagbark Hickory (*Carya ovata*) and Yellow Birch (*Betula lutea*). Conifers form 20-80 percent of the canopy in this area, which is quintessentially mixed conifer-hardwood forest.

The understory and herbaceous flora of the forest are characteristic of habitats found further to the north. The Hobblebush (*Viburnum alnifolium*) is a conspicuous, large-leaved component of the understory, which drops out of the forest community south of this spot. Its spectacular white clusters of flowers fill the forest in late May. It is joined on the steep, rocky, but moist and more fertile lower slopes of the hollow by species like Striped Maple (*A. pensylvanicum*), Red Elderberry (*Sambucus pubens*), Canada Honeysuckle (*Lonicera canadensis*), Mapleleaf Viburnum (*V. acerifolium*), Flowering Dogwood (*Cornus florida*) and extensive patches of Mountain Laurel (*Kalmia latifolia*).

The herbaceous flora of the west slope of Boston Hollow is

reminiscent of the wildflower gardens that can be found in spring at high elevation slopes in the southern Appalachian Mountains. In May, a profusion of wildflower species like Round-lobed Hepatica (*Hepatica americana*), Bloodroot (*Sanguinaria canadensis*), Wood Anemone (*Anemone quinquefolia*), Wild Lily-of-the-valley (*Maianthemum canadense*), Solomon's Seal (*Polygonatum biflorum*), False Solomon's Seal (*Smilicina racemosa*), Red Trillium (*Trillium erectum*), Blue Cohosh (*Caulophyllum thalictroides*), Red Baneberry (*Actea rubra*), White Baneberry (*A. alba*), Jack-in-the-Pulpit (*Arisaema triphyllum*), Trailing Arbutus (*Epigaea repens*) and Dwarf Ginseng (*Panax trifolium*) can be found. Moreover, species characteristic of more northern environments, like Clintonia (*Clintonia borealis*), Round-leaved Yellow Violet (*Viola rotundifolia*), Bunchberry (*Cornus canadensis*) and Goldthread (*Coptis groenlandica*) are present.

The fern flora on the lower slopes is also a rich one. One of the more interesting species present is the ephemeral Fragile Fern (*Cystopteris fragilis*), which dies back by mid-late summer as conditions become drier. It may be found growing from cracks in larger boulders, as may another rock-associated species, the Common Polypody (*Polypodium vulgare*). In this same area the delicate and lacy Maidenhair Fern (*Adiantum pedatum*) is fairly common as well. Other typical ferns of the lower slopes include the Lady Fern (*Athyrium filix-femina*), Spinulose Wood Fern (*Dryopteris spinulosa*), Marginal Shield Fern (*D. marginalis*), New York Fern (*Thelypteris noveboracensis*) and Christmas Fern (*Polystichum acrostichoides*).

As the trail ascends the slope, patches of largely pure hemlock-pine stands are encountered, but above these the forest becomes dry and deciduous, and it is dominated by species like Chestnut Oak, (*Q. prinus*), Huckleberry (*Gaylussacia baccata*) and Bracken Fern (*Pteridium aquilinum*). Although this type of forest is not the focus of the present field trip, ascending to the ridge top affords a view of the surrounding countryside. From the summit, the unbroken extent of the forest is evident. In winter, the frequency with which conifers are present in this southernmost tongue of northern forest is conspicuous. The gleaming white trunks of the forest's numerous White Birches (*B. papyrifera*), another characteristic tree of the north woods, are also conspicuous at this season.

A swampy stream borders the base of Boston Hollow. This stream exhibits mixed forest cover. Eastern Hemlock and Eastern White Pine are at home not only in uplands, but also on hummocks (high spots formed from the rotting, moss-covered roots of fallen trees) in swamps. Common associates of these conifers include Red Maple, Yellow Birch, Black Ash (*F. nigra*) and a dense shrub layer composed of species like Mountain Laurel, Winterberry (*Ilex verticillata*), Mountain Holly (*Nemopanthus mucronata*), Highbush Blueberry (*Vaccinium corymbosum*), Speckled Alder (*Alnus rugosa*) and Sweet Pepper Bush (*Clethra alnifolia*).

Wildlife: Boston Hollow has a rich reptile and amphibian fauna. The wetland supports populations of the Northern Dusky and Northern Two-lined Salamanders as well as Green, Bull and Pickerel Frogs. Moreover, the Spotted Salamander, American Toad, Wood Frog, Spring Peeper and Gray Tree Frog all come to its waters to breed. In the adjacent uplands, the Red-backed Salamander is abundant, the Wood Frog is common, and I have occasionally found Wood Turtles in moister upland forests. The rare Northern Spring Salamander has been found in the vicinity.

Spotted Salamander

The diverse bird life in the Boston Hollow area is legendary among local birdwatchers. It is possible to find 100 species of birds in the immediate vicinity on a single spring day. Included in this total are over 30 species of wood warblers, as well as some of the region's less common migrants. An open swamp at the north end of the hollow has been a good place for finding rarities like the Olive-sided Flycatcher in spring and fall, as well as Purple Martins and even Cliff Swallows.

Numerous species remain to breed, including some that are at or near their southern range limit. The wetland and its adjacent borders along the base of the hollow support nesting populations of the Louisiana and Northern Waterthrush, Canada Warbler, Veery, Eastern Phoebe, Winter Wren and Acadian Flycatcher. The adjacent upland forests have breeding populations of the Northern Goshawk, Red-shouldered Hawk, Pileated Woodpecker, Eastern Wood Pewee, Great-crested Flycatcher, Wood Thrush, Scarlet Tanager, Red-eyed Vireo, Blue-headed Vireo, Ovenbird and Dark-eyed Junco. In patches of conifers, Red-breasted Nuthatches, Blackburnian Warblers and Black-throated Green Warblers are present. On the drier upper slopes, the Black-throated Blue Warbler and Hermit Thrush are regular nesters. During one spring, a territorial Swainson's Thrush, a species generally absent with us in summer, remained on these slopes until early June. Some of Connecticut's first nesting Common Ravens appeared in Boston Hollow, and other local rarities like breeding Pine Siskins, Golden-crowned Kinglets and White-throated Sparrows have appeared in the area as well.

As productive as spring and summer outings to Boston Hollow can be, winter trips to the area can also be most instructive. One notable feature that I have observed repeatedly is the area's *lack* of wintering birds. In fact, when I mapped the density and diversity of

Veery nest

winter bird communities across eastern Connecticut, I consistently found that the entire Northeast Uplands Ecoregion had low bird populations. My initial interpretation was that the harsher winter conditions in this area make it less attractive to wintering birds. Birds are dramatically more dense and diverse in southern Connecticut, where winters average substantially milder.

Despite the low density and variety of birds present in winter, there are still some specialties that may be found at this season. The abundant conifers make the forests attractive to northern finch species that appear with us primarily in winter. Species like the Pine Siskin, Red Crossbill, White-winged Crossbill and Common Redpoll all appear here. The coniferous wetland is also a place where species like the Saw-whet Owl roost.

A substantial variety of mammals are present in the Boston Hollow area, including some species at their southern range limit. Northern Flying Squirrels, for example, have been found in the vicinity. Moreover, when the more northerly distributed Fisher began recolonizing Connecticut in the 1970s, I first found it at Boston Hollow. More recently, the Black Bear and Moose have begun ranging south into this area. I have seen as well a clear photograph of a Mountain Lion reportedly taken in nearby Union.

Inhabitants of the Boston Hollow wetland include the Red-backed Vole, Beaver, Mink and, occasionally, River Otter. The adjacent uplands are occupied by species like the Red and Gray Squirrels, Chipmunk, White-footed Mouse, Bobcat, Gray Fox and Raccoon. The Coyote is now also a regular inhabitant of the area. Even the occasional Groundhog makes its home among the steeply rocky slopes, in a manner reminiscent of its Rocky Mountain cousin, the Yellowbelly Marmot. Moreover, Porcupines were common in the area in the 1970s, and numerous mounds of their characteristic fiber-filled droppings were present in surrounding forests. However, since the appearance of its predator, the Fisher, it seems to have declined greatly in the area.

Closing thoughts: A notable historic feature of Boston Hollow is a tiny abandoned mine present near the hollow's southern end. Legend has it that the rocks were mined for non-existent gold after an unscrupulous individual seeded the area with several specks of the metal.

The principal area where conifer-northern hardwood forest is common in eastern Connecticut is comparatively small. It extends from west Woodstock to central Stafford, and south to north Ashford. Within this region, however, there are excellent areas for observing conifer-northern hardwood forest. Bigelow Hollow State Park in Union possesses fine examples of the habitat. Moreover, the Nipmuck Trail passes through the 8,000 acres of Yale Experimental Forest as well as through Nipmuck State Forest. Along much of the trail's length in the Union-Ashford area mixed forest prevails.

Much more extensive regions of conifer-northern hardwood forest are found in the steeply hilly landscapes of Northwest Connecticut. Places like Macedonia Brook State Park in Kent, Canaan Mountain in North Canaan, and Algonquin State Forest in Colebrook all possess conifer-northern hardwood forest. However, even at these places local conditions control whether the forested landscape has developed into this or another forest type.

Pine-Oak Forest 9

Pine-oak forests are largely associated with drier and poorer soils in Connecticut. Eastern White Pine is the commonest pine to occur with oaks, although Pitch Pine is common as well, and often the two pines co-occur. Pine-oak forests are found throughout the state, although they are particularly common in southeastern Connecticut near the Rhode Island border, where they are contiguous with more extensive areas of such forests east of our border. Other notable expanses are found in the Connecticut River Valley.

These forests often develop on sand and gravel that was deposited at the close of the glacial era. Glaciers left materials throughout Connecticut, and these materials may be classified into two principal types. One is ice laid deposits, which include till (various types of sands, gravels and rocks left as a covering at many locations) and end moraines. Moraines are areas that formed along the southern edge of the glacier where piles of debris collected over time. The best-developed end moraines are approximately contiguous with the present Connecticut shoreline.

The other principal classification of glacier-associated materials is that of meltwater deposits. These are materials carried by streams of melting water flowing from glaciers, primarily into valleys. Many meltwater deposits accumulated in the basins of temporary lakes, called glacial lakes, which formed as ice retreated north. A number of large glacial lakes existed in Connecticut with the biggest, Lake Hitchcock, occupying much of what is now the upper Connecticut River Valley. Another, Lake Middletown, occurred south of Lake Hitchcock. Still others occurred in western Connecticut, and a cluster of five occurred near the Rhode Island border.

One of Connecticut's less common habitats is often closely associated with meltwater deposits. This habitat is dominated by Pitch Pine, a species that tends to invade sandy areas after they are disturbed. Such habitats are widespread in southeastern Massachusetts, Rhode Island, Long Island and southern New Jersey. Pitch Pine likely occurred

Pine barrens

more extensively in Connecticut during pre-European times when native people burned large areas of the landscape. Sandy soils left by glaciers and present along the coast, in parts of the Connecticut River Valley and in southeastern Connecticut all likely supported extensive examples of this habitat. Today, stands still may be found in these areas, although in many instances oaks are replacing Pitch Pines as forests mature.

Pitch Pine possesses several adaptations that make it successful in periodically burned landscapes. Its cones are referred to as serotinous, which means they open when exposed to the type of heat generated by wildfires. Seeds broadcast by opening cones germinate well in the bare mineral soil left by fires. Moreover, burned trees can send out new growth directly from the trunk and major branches. In contrast, fire suppresses Pitch Pine's competitors, the oaks. The kind of Pitch Pine-oak forests that develop in these disturbed areas are often referred to as "pine barrens," because they are open and scrubby in character.

Conditions conducive to the production of wildfires persist today in places like the New Jersey pine barrens. Fires natural in origin and human-caused continue to burn the highly flammable pine barrens community. The extensive white sands of the region are said to reflect heat so effectively that they can spontaneously start fires. I have indeed been present in this habitat on July days when the reflected heat alone was sufficient to open Pitch Pine cones. In regions within the pine barrens where fires occur every ten years or less, a community called pine plains develops. This dwarf community grows to only three or four feet in height.

In Connecticut, in contrast, fire is a rarely occurring part of the forest ecosystem. In fact, plant ecologists consider the prevailing mature, deciduous forest of our region to be largely fireproof under natural circumstances. With us, new stands of Pitch Pine often appear to begin in response to mechanical disturbance like logging. Without frequent fire, Connecticut has only small examples of pine barrens habitat and no pine plains communities. However, areas referred to as sand plains occasionally develop.

Sand plains are successional environments (see chapter on successional habitats) that develop on glacial sand deposits after some form of disturbance. Sandy soil tends to be poor at holding water and nutrients, and only species tolerant of such dry and sterile conditions colonize these areas. Typically, sand plains exhibit scattered clumps of Pitch Pine growing with an understory of Scrub Oak. Other oaks, particularly Black, White and Scarlet Oak also invade and become more prevalent as these areas mature. Clumps of trees or individual trees may be in otherwise open areas. These openings can be vegetated by Little Bluestem grass or have little vegetative cover. Unvegetated areas instead can be populated by especially lichens and mosses, which grow on the surface of the characteristically spongy soil. Because growing conditions are poor, these areas may change comparatively slowly with time.

FIELD TRIP
Mansfield Hollow State Park, Mansfield-Windham

Directions: Several areas within Mansfield Hollow are worth visiting. One may be reached by traveling north on Rt. 6 in Windham and parking on the left just north of Windham airport. This lot affords access to a walkway atop Mansfield Hollow Dam. Another area may be reached by traveling further north on Rt. 6 to the junction of Basset's Bridge Rd. Turn left onto this road, cross over the Natchaug River, and immediately turn left onto Old North Windham Rd. This road leads to a parking lot and gated road that can be explored on foot. By returning to Basset's Bridge Rd. and traveling further west, a third parking area is reached where the road crosses over the lake. Park here and look for the blue dots of the Nipmuck Trail, which can be followed along the edge of the lake.

Equipment: No special equipment is needed to walk the roads and trails of Mansfield Hollow, although I find that hiking boots are always the best choice when walking in the forest. Ticks, mosquitoes and black flies are present at certain times of the year, so long pants, socks, long sleeve shirts, hats and insect repellent are also wise choices.   Binoculars and field guides are helpful.

The habitat: Mansfield Hollow is one of the regions in Connecticut where extensive glacial meltwater deposits may be found. Much of the soil of the region is sandy and gravelly, and these soils have given rise to several types of pine-oak communities. The least common one is a sand plain, much of which appears to have developed in response to disturbance caused by the construction of Mansfield Hollow Dam in the early 1950s. This area may be reached from the Rt. 6 parking lot by using the paved walkway atop Mansfield Hollow Dam. It may be observed directly from the walkway. When I first began visiting this small area in the early 1970s, it was still heavily disturbed from various forms of human activity. Since that time, it has been gated and fenced so that the effects of disturbance have diminished.

Over much of the site, Pitch Pine (*P. rigida*) is the dominant tree species, although it is joined by White (*Quercus alba*), Black (*Q. velutina*) and Scarlet Oak (*Q. coccinea*) in the canopy of

Pitch Pine sand plain

wooded areas. In some areas the oaks predominate. Trees like Gray Birch (*Betula populifolia*), Eastern Redcedar (*Juniperus virginiana*) and Quaking Aspen (*Populus tremuloides*), often referred to as pioneer species, or species that are among the first to colonize a disturbed area, are also present. The understory consists of saplings of the same oak species, along with the shrubby species Scrub Oak (*Quercus ilicifolia*). Copses of trees are bordered by areas sparsely vegetated by shrubs and grasses. Several shrubs typical of dry, sandy areas are found here, including Common Juniper (*J. communis*), Sweet Fern (*Myrica asplenifolia*), Lowbush Blueberry (*Vaccinium angustifolium*) and New Jersey Tea (*Ceanothus americana*). A sparse cover of the grass Little Bluestem (*Andropogon scoparius*) dominates the most open areas. Also abundant in these open areas are various types of mosses and lichens.

Since the 1970s this area has matured somewhat, although the speed of maturation has been rather low, as might be expected in the poor soils of this area. Pitch Pine and Little Bluestem were abundant in the 1970s and they remain so. Since disturbance has been reduced, areas that were bare sand have become covered with bluestem, lichens and moss. Moreover, oaks have become increasingly important, as they have matured from saplings into the woodland canopy. Presently, the area is undergoing some management. Oaks have been logged from part of the area. However, because the area is a successional environment, that is, one that is in the process of maturing to forest, one might question whether management to maintain the area in its present state is a valid procedure, as successional environments are by their nature dynamic systems.

Other Pitch Pine-oak associations dot the Mansfield Hollow area. A more mature stand in which Pitch Pine dominates may be found along an old paved road leading from the Old North Windham Rd. parking lot. Also present in this area are stands in which Eastern White Pine predominates.

An extensive example of our more widespread forest community, Eastern White Pine (*Pinus strobus*) -Pitch Pine-oak forest, may be explored from the Basset's Bridge parking lot. The blue dot trail passes through several largely pure pine stands, and then enters pine-oak forest. In addition to the two pine species, White, Black and Scarlet Oak are again important forest constituents, along with Red Maple (*Acer rubrum*). In the forest understory, species like Huckleberry (*Gaylussacia baccata*), Round-leaved Blueberry (*V. vacillans*) and Bracken Fern (*Pteridium aquilinum*) are particularly common. These are rather mature forests, and I have measured in them pines and oaks with diameters to 28 inches.

Wildlife: There are fewer kinds of reptiles and amphibians in upland pine-oak forests than in moister situations. However, a number of species are still present. The ubiquitous Red-backed Salamander may be found under leaf litter, under rocks and under fallen logs. Moreover, the only specimen of a Worm Snake I have ever seen came from sandy environments like those typical of pine-oak forest.

A notable feature of the Mansfield Hollow area is the presence of glacial kettle holes. These areas formed when blocks of glacial ice melted, leaving a depression in the ground. Such depressions often fill with water in spring. The vernal (temporary) pools formed in kettle holes are among the most important breeding habitats for a number of spring breeding amphibians. Because vernal pools are generally unconnected to more permanent bodies of water, they lack some of the predators like fish that occur in permanent water. This reduction in predators improves the probability of survival by amphibian eggs and larvae (juvenile hatchling stages). The Spotted Salamander, Wood Frog, Spring Peeper, Gray Tree Frog, American Toad and Fowler's Toad all breed in these pools. Another species, the Marbled Salamander, also breeds in pools like these, although it does so in fall rather than spring.

Bird life of the pine-oak forest includes some species that are typical of it. The Pine Warbler is a species more frequent in pure pine stands, but it also occurs fairly commonly in forests where clumps of pines are present or where pines are at least regular components of the forest canopy. At Mansfield Hollow, the high, extended trill of summering Pine Warblers is a characteristic sound, although the song can be confused with two other species also present in the area. The Worm-eating Warbler, also common at Mansfield Hollow, has an extremely similar song, but lives in the forest understory, whereas the Pine Warbler is an inhabitant of treetops. Both, however, may be heard singing from the same group of trees. Still another species with a very similar song is the Chipping Sparrow. Although this species is more typical of forest openings and forest edge, both it and the Pine Warbler may be heard singing from the tops of the same white pines. Considerable practice is needed to master distinguishing among the songs of these species.

While performing large-scale surveys of habitat use by forest birds in Connecticut, I found few species that occurred in pine-oak forest more than would be predicted by chance. The few included summering Blue Jays, winter and summer populations of Brown Creepers, and breeding Yellow-rumped Warblers. A variety of other species occurred in these forests as well, but did not preferentially occupy them. Typical inhabitants included the Eastern Wood Pewee, Hermit Thrush, Scarlet Tanager, Ovenbird and Black-and-

Hermit Thrush

white Warbler. Still another occasional resident of the mature pine-oak forests of the Mansfield Hollow area is the Northern Goshawk. During summer, care should be taken not to disturb nesting goshawks, which will vigorously defend the nest site against intruders, including people.

In sand plain habitats, the often scattered clumps of conifers favor some species but discourage others more characteristic of forest interiors. The Pine Warbler is again present, and it is joined by species like the Prairie and Blue-winged Warblers. The Rufous-sided Towhee and Gray Catbird also inhabit areas of forest edge and thickets.

Because the sand plain at Mansfield Hollow is directly adjacent to the Windham Airport, several kinds of birds that inhabit open country also may be found in the vicinity. The airport, like the sand plain and pine-oak forests of the vicinity, sits upon sand and gravel deposits. The sparse grass covering the area simulates conditions in western grasslands, and because of the area's extent and the fact that some portions are only occasionally mowed, it is attractive for grassland-nesting birds. Species like the Killdeer, Horned Lark, Savannah Sparrow and Grasshopper Sparrow all summer there. On occasion, the Vesper Sparrow has been present as well. Once I even found the usually tundra nesting Water Pipit acting as if it were seeking a nest site, although in this instance I don't think it ultimately remained to breed.

Mammals of the pine-oak forest are not notably distinct from those of other types of forest. The only small mammal I have found more common in these types of woodlands is, not surprisingly based on its name, the Pine Vole. It is a species that is also the bane of fruit growers, as it has a propensity for gnawing the bark from sapling fruit trees, thereby killing them. I kept one in captivity for a time, and found it was unusual among small mammals in its requirements for drinking large amounts of water. I found I constantly had to refill its water bottle in order to keep it supplied.

In contrast, its rodent relatives, the White-footed Mouse and Meadow Vole, required little care. Also unlike the Meadow Vole, which can be quite tame in captivity, at least the Pine Voles I have kept have been rather belligerent.

I once briefly kept small mammals in captivity to observe them, but since the rabies epidemic of the 1990s I have stopped. Rodents can carry diseases transmissible to people. The dangers associated with them have become too significant to handle them.

Among other mammals that may be found in pine-oak habitats, the White-footed Mouse is the typical upland forest mouse, whereas the Meadow Vole is the characteristic species inhabiting forest openings. In sand plains, the Meadow Vole inhabits more open areas vegetated by grasses and shrubs. In forested areas, both the Gray and Red Squirrels may be found, with the Gray Squirrel more typical of deciduous forest and the Red Squirrel most closely associated with groups of pines.

Closing thoughts: It is possible to find pine-oak forests most anywhere in Connecticut. Extensive examples are found at Kollar Wildlife Management Area in Tolland, as well as in the Pachaug State Forest area around Voluntown. Pitch Pine-oak forests and sand plain habitats are more limited in extent, but examples exist at several places. In the town of Sterling, there are several areas where Pitch Pine is abundant. Moreover, along the Sterling-Rhode Island border at Pachaug State Forest there is an extensive area of scrubby, open Pitch Pine-oak barrens that has developed on the extremely poor soils. Oaks predominate in this habitat, but the overall effect is of maturing pine barrens. Still other areas of Pitch Pine-oak habitats are found in the Enfield vicinity. Enfield was once at the bottom of glacial Lake Hitchcock. The sandy-gravelly deposits left from the former lake are vegetated in places by Pitch Pine-oak. A final example is at Rocky Neck State Park, East Lyme. Pitch Pine-oak forests are thought to have been extensive along the coast in areas of terminal moraine deposits. Tiny remnants of this forest type may be found adjacent to tidal wetlands in the park.

Conifer Forest 10

Conifers are comparatively primitive plants of ancient lineage. They predate the flowering plants, and during the time of the dinosaurs they were the predominant forest trees. Botanists call the conifers gymnosperms, which means naked-seeded. Unlike the flowering plants, which bear their seeds within a fruit, conifer seeds develop naked on the scales of cones, although certain conifers produce fruit-like structures.

The days of a Connecticut landscape covered by extensive conifer forests are long since past. The most recent tenure of widespread conifer cover in our region was rather brief from a geological perspective. Forests like those found today in northern Maine and in the higher elevations of the White and Green Mountains began to establish themselves in Connecticut about 14,000 years ago, only several thousand years after glacial ice had retreated north. However, global climate warmed rapidly, and by 10,000 years ago the conifers were being replaced by forests more like those presently found in northwestern Connecticut and Massachusetts.

Red Spruce

Today, the remains of those earlier conifer forests are restricted to few spots. One might think of their retreat much like the retreat of snow after a spring thaw. The uniform snow cover breaks into patches, and these become progressively confined to shady spots and other cooler microclimates, until at last only a few patches remain. We are at this stage with our northern-associated (boreal) conifer forest today. Its characteristic components are Red Spruce, Balsam Fir and Red Pine in the uplands, and Northern White-cedar, Black Spruce and Tamarack in wetter areas.

The upland spruce-fir forests typical of the far north are in Connecticut restricted to small stands, primarily in the northwestern corner of the state, and are often associated with the colder microclimates around bogs. One of the species of these forests, Balsam Fir, is rather rare as a native although it is widely planted and may appear virtually anywhere in the state. As a wild tree it occurs sparingly in northwestern Connecticut. The Northern White-cedar also is a rare native that occurs on upland limestone soils and at the edges of bogs. Like Balsam Fir, it is widely planted, which clouds its status as a naturally occurring species. Red Pine is still another rare native that appears to occur naturally only in northwestern Connecticut. It is also widely planted, although since the 1970s planted stands have suffered heavy mortality from insect pests. In contrast to these species, Black Spruce is more widespread but restricted to bogs and swamps. It is found primarily in northern Connecticut, where it frequently co-occurs with our only deciduous (leaves are lost in autumn) conifer, Tamarack.

The Eastern White Pine and Eastern Hemlock are conifers that can be important components of northern forests, although they are not restricted to the far north and high mountains like the previous species. Both are major components of Connecticut's forests, particularly in the northern half of the state. They may co-occur or grow as single species stands.

Eastern White Pine is the monarch of the eastern forest. Specimens to 220 feet tall and 6 feet in diameter have been recorded. Trees may attain an age of greater than 450 years, and do not even reach maturity (the age at which growth greatly slows) until they are 200 years old. It is an extremely valuable timber tree that makes rapid growth on better soils. Consequently, it is widely planted in single species stands. It is moderately tolerant of competition and can invade stands of oaks, but it becomes most abundant in areas that have been disturbed. Its seeds germinate well in places where the forest canopy has been removed, and in such areas it can grow into largely pure stands. Most of our state's pure conifer forests are white pine forests.

Eastern Hemlock is one of Connecticut's longest-lived trees.

The largest specimen I have found in Connecticut was 40 inches in diameter and 100 feet tall, although I have seen even larger individuals in virgin stands elsewhere. Specimens in excess of 600 years of age, 160 feet tall and 7 feet in diameter have been reported. Unlike Eastern White Pine, it is extremely tolerant of shade and competition from other species, and its seeds germinate in the organic soils characteristic of mature forest interiors. Hence, it is a species that becomes an important constituent of old growth communities. Although it can be found in a variety of situations, it makes its best growth and can become an overwhelming dominant in moist coves, such as occur bordering streams.

Despite its competitive strengths, Eastern Hemlock has been catastrophically affected by an introduced insect pest and is now largely eliminated from forests across southern portions of the state. Northern Connecticut populations are suffering mortality as well, although as yet their destruction has not been so complete.

Several other species of conifers also can form pure stands with us. All are associated with disturbance. The Pitch Pine is usually a smaller, poorly formed tree, although it can attain an age of 200 years and height of 100 feet. It occurs most frequently on sandy, dry, sterile soils. It establishes itself well after disturbance, particularly fire, but is replaced by other species like oaks as the forest matures.

Pitch Pine reaches its greatest abundance in regions where sandy soils predominate, such as the pine barrens of southern New Jersey, eastern Long Island and southeastern Massachusetts. Rhode Island formerly had extensive stands of Pitch Pine, but these are being replaced by oaks as its forests mature. In Connecticut, small stands of Pitch Pine have developed particularly in the southeastern portion of the state where glacial activity has left extensive deposits of sand and gravel. Pitch Pine stands are also present on rocky, sterile hilltops, and on areas of sand deposits in the Connecticut River Valley.

Still another conifer associated with disturbance is the Eastern Redcedar. It typically colonizes maturing old fields (see chapter on successional habitats) along with other pioneer tree species (species that are the first to colonize an area) like Quaking Aspen and Gray Birch, although on occasion it can form pure stands. It is a slow growing tree that makes its best growth on richer soils, but it is often more predominant on poorer, sandy areas. Despite its being a pioneer tree, it can attain an age of 300 years. However, it is intolerant of competition from other tree species, which overtop it in maturing old fields. Once shaded by larger trees, it eventually dies. In developing woodlands around Connecticut, the gaunt skeletons of dead Eastern Redcedars occur commonly beneath the forest canopy.

The Atlantic White-cedar is one last conifer species that occurs with us. Like the previous two species, it can form pure stands, particularly after disturbance. However, it is restricted to wetlands, so it is discussed at greater length under the heading of swamps.

FIELD TRIP
Pachaug State Forest, Voluntown

Directions: There are many possible approaches to the extensive Pachaug State Forest. A favorite spot may be reached by traveling east on Rt. 138 to its junction with Rt. 49. Travel north on Rt. 49 for about one mile, and turn left at the State Forest sign. A number of dirt roads traverse the area, and all allow exploration of the forest, although some are closed in winter. On foot, the blue dot (Pachaug) trail is a good one to follow. It may be found by traveling on the dirt road that leads from the park entrance, and looking for the blue dot trail markers. Park opposite the sign for the Rhododendron sanctuary and begin walking the trail there.

Equipment: No special equipment is needed to walk the dirt roads and trails of the Pachaug area, although I find that hiking boots are always the best choice when walking in the forest. Ticks, mosquitoes and black flies are present at certain times of the year, so long pants, socks, long sleeve shirts, hats and insect repellent are also wise choices. Binoculars and field guides are helpful. Although most area trails traverse rather flat ground, some are rather steep and rocky, so take special precautions on wet days to avoid slipping on the rocks.

The habitat: Pachaug State Forest is one of the largest public holdings in the state. It is spread over the towns of Sterling, Plainfield, Voluntown, Griswold and North Stonington. It is also contiguous with the vast Arcadia Management Area in adjacent Rhode Island, so is part of one of southern New England's better preserved ecosystem. In many regards the Pachaug area, with its frequently sandy and poor soils, is more like neighboring Rhode Island than much of the rest of Connecticut.

Pure conifer forests are widespread within Pachaug State Forest. They are largely planted, although some naturally occurring conifer associations are found as well. The road into the forest passes extensive examples of planted Eastern White Pines (*Pinus strobus*). Red Pine (*P. resinosa*) stands were once common in the area, but most have been logged in the aftermath of disease. Stands of the boreal Canadian species, White Spruce (*Picea glauca*), are also planted, as are stands of the elegant, drooping-branched European native, Norway Spruce (*P. abies*). One additional species that is planted quite commonly is the European Larch (*Larix decidua*). Like its native relative Tamarack (*L. laricina*), it loses its leaves in fall. Unlike Tamarack, however, it is a large tree of upland environments.

The Rocky Mountain native, Douglas-fir (*Pseudotsuga menziesii*), is another species planted in some areas of the forest. One of the most important timber trees in North America, it is not related to true firs. The papery bracts that extend out of its cones distinguish it from any other conifer. Still another Rocky Mountain species that is sometimes planted is the White Fir (*Abies concolor*). This handsome, silvery-leaved species is a true fir.

Old growth Eastern Hemlock

Unlike the spruces, which have cones that hang down and are persistent on the tree, this and other firs have upright cones that disintegrate at maturity.

An interesting side trip to take while on the blue dot trail is to the Rhododendron sanctuary. A short side trail leads through a fine example of a mature Atlantic White-cedar (*Chamaecyparis thyoides*) swamp with a Rhododendron (*Rhododendron maximum*) understory, which will be discussed in greater detail in the chapter on swamps. Continuing west, the trail passes through a mature Eastern Hemlock (*Tsuga canadensis*) –Eastern White Pine forest in which, as of this writing, the hemlocks remain alive. Trees have diameters of up to 23 inches and, as is typical of these types of forests, there is little understory shrubbery or herbaceous growth.

Continuing on the trail up Mount Misery, still another largely pure conifer stand occurs. The dry, rocky summit has a small Pitch Pine (*P. rigida*)-Scrub Oak (*Quercus ilicifolia*) community. Pitch Pine is a frequent inhabitant of ridge tops like this one. It is also found fairly commonly as an individual tree in many of the forests of the Pachaug region. A more extensive Pitch Pine community, which includes such typical pine barrens shrubs as the sprawling Bearberry (*Arctostaphlos uva-ursi*), occurs just a short drive further east from Pachaug along Rt. 165 into Exeter, Rhode Island. Another typical pine barrens species, Smooth Holly (*Ilex glabra*), is present rarely in the Pachaug area, although it becomes fairly common further east near the Rhode Island shore.

Wildlife: The highly acidic leaf litter beneath conifer stands is not particularly notable for supporting a variety of amphibians and reptiles, although certain species can occur there. Those typical of the sandy soils underlying many pine-dominated landscapes are the Fowler's Toad and Eastern Hognose Snake. The latter preys upon the toads. Another species, the Eastern Spadefoot, is extremely rare in Connecticut, but it is known to inhabit sandy environments in the Pachaug area.

The bird life of conifer forests is quite distinctive, and includes species largely restricted to these habitats. One, the Pine Warbler, is found in areas dominated by Eastern White or Pitch Pine. It appears to have become increasingly common in the past few decades, and now has a center of abundance in the Pachaug area. The Black-throated Green Warbler is also rather widespread, although it tends to occur more frequently in the hemlock-white pine associations of northern Connecticut. Less widespread but found as well in hemlock-white pine forests are several typically boreal species, the Red-breasted Nuthatch, Blackburnian Warbler and Yellow-rumped Warbler. In disturbed areas regenerating with young conifers, the Nashville and Magnolia Warblers may be found, although both are rather uncommon here at the southern extremity of their range. In pine barrens habitats, the Prairie Warbler and Rufous-sided Towhee join with the Pine Warbler as characteristic species.

Winter can bring its own suite of primarily conifer-associated birds. The Red Crossbill and White-winged Crossbill are irregular winter visitors that wander south in years when the conifer seed crop across the far north is poor. More consistent winter migrants into Connecticut are the Pine Siskin and Common Redpoll, although neither is as closely associated with conifer habitats as the crossbills. Wintering Saw-whet and Long-eared Owls use conifer stands as roosts.

The most characteristic mammalian inhabitant of conifer forests is the Red Squirrel. It is one of the few mammal species that actively defends a territory against others of its species. Unlike many kinds of birds, most mammals are unable to defend territories because the costs of defending them are too high (e.g. many calories must be expended to patrol the boundaries of an area on foot). However, the density of cones and seeds in a conifer grove can be great enough so that these squirrels are able to effectively defend them.

Red Squirrel

Closing thoughts: Fine examples of mature hemlock and white pine stands may still be found in Bigelow Hollow State Park in Union, Furnace Brook State Park in Killingly, Macedonia Brook State Park in Kent, and a number of other spots across northern Connecticut. The once magnificent hemlock ravines of Devil's Hopyard State Park in East Haddam and the Byram River in Greenwich are now gone, however. A particularly spectacular stand of old growth Eastern White Pine may be seen at Gold's Pines, which is on Rt. 128 in West Cornwall. Trees in excess of 200 years old populate a small area thought to have been abandoned in the 1700's. Other mature stands of white pine may be seen at White Memorial Foundation in Litchfield and Yale Forest in Union.

Coastal Woodlands 11

In 1934, Lieutenant Gordon Armes, U.S. Cavalry, signed the honorable discharge of my father from military service. By doing so, Armes had participated in the close of an era. The cavalry was no more, and before long much of what had transpired during those military years similarly would be confined to the realm of receding memory.

At age 18 years, 11 months, Pop had entered military service during the beginning years of the Great Depression. He was assigned to Panama, where he volunteered to explore the unknown and still virgin wilderness of central Panama. In the 18th century the English buccaneer Sir Henry Morgan had hacked a trail through the region, but it had remained largely unexplored since. Pop was charged with relocating the remains of that trail, and for the rest of his life his favorite stories were of the untouched jungle, dripping with boa constrictors, infested with malaria, and populated by Indian tribes with little knowledge of the outside world.

But that time became the past, and its forests and secrets are now gone. Little tangible remains. I have some photographs, and an Indian knife with a history I wish it could relate, but little else, save for a kernel of the less tangible. I am hard pressed to remember any time when I did not know of those forests that I could never visit. That knowledge left me with a private longing to know such places; to discover if on the ground where they once stood there were any secrets left to learn. This is where my story begins.

In 1912, the year my father was born, there still existed in Stonington, Connecticut a stand of old forest, a sliver of what the first European explorers to this region would have seen. While rummaging through old literature during my last year of graduate school, a perennial

James Craig, Panama, 1932

favorite pastime of mine, I chanced across several long forgotten articles about this site. It was studied by Yale botanist George Nichols, who described it in 1913 as part of his comprehensive analysis of Connecticut vegetation. The stand persisted until the fall of 1938, when the great hurricane of that year made landfall almost precisely over it. A year later, Harvard botanist Hugh Raup returned to the area, and chronicled the status of its remains. Afterwards, like the boas of primeval Panama, it too became a fading memory.

Nichols reported that the forest was unusual for old growth in that the dominant trees were oak and hickory rather than the beech-birch-maple-hemlock more typical of southern New England old growth. Moreover, it was more open in character than typical forests of the region. He speculated that partial clearing may have occurred at some point in the past, but could draw no firm conclusions.

The hurricane-ravaged site visited by Raup 27 years after Nichols helped to provide some of the missing evidence for the stand's history. Raup had the opportunity to examine stumps from wind-thrown trees. Stumps show annual growth rings, and the number of these rings determines a tree's age. Moreover, the ring's width records how rapidly a tree grew during a particular year. He found that there were two groups of stumps. One exhibited over 140 growth rings, and showed a sudden widening of rings about the year 1815, the time of the last catastrophic hurricane. Such widening indicated accelerated growth due to release from competition with other trees. The other group was less than 140 years old and did not exhibit the sudden widening. Most trees appeared to have begun growing after 1815.

I endured a year of curiosity about the Stonington site before finally succumbing, and in the summer of 1976 set about trying to determine where the forest had been. Armed with topographic maps and my predecessor's descriptions, I narrowed the search to a hill near Long Island Sound. After talking with local landowners, I gained permission to explore the site, which remains in private ownership.

During my exploration, I found that the area had become thickly forested with sapling trees all of about the same age. Foresters refer to this as a dense, even-aged stand. Near a road I also found a recently cut Black Birch stump with 70 growth rings. Its rings from about 35 years earlier showed a sudden widening. This suggested that the smaller, even-aged trees had begun growing about 35 years ago, or shortly after the time of the 1938 hurricane. However, in exploring the site I also found nine much larger trees, with the largest, a White Oak, having a diameter of nearly three feet. Other giants were a Pignut Hickory of 31 inches, a Red Maple of 29 inches, and Sassafras of 25 inches. The Sassafras struck me particularly. I had never before (or since) seen a specimen of this generally smaller species with such titanic proportions.

I also found an old oak stump with a 17-inch diameter and 109 growth rings. This decayed stump appeared to be a remnant of post-1938 logging of downed trees, as its age corresponded well with those reported by Raup. Based on this stump, I estimated that the largest remaining trees were 110 years to 160 years old, and that the largest few trees were perhaps older still. Another notable feature of the large trees was that they had spreading growth forms, consistent with the type of growth expected if they had developed in the open forest described by Nichols.

As chance would have it, I had the opportunity to directly observe the effects of a comparatively weak hurricane on this area only several weeks after making my initial observations. This storm made landfall in southeastern Connecticut. Within a week, the toxic effects of salt spray on leaves could be seen extending inland for miles.

I have contemplated this forest since. In its location, composition and characteristics, it was clear that I had found

Nichols' lost stand. But what of its history? Nichols was unsure whether it was truly "virgin," in part because he observed the forest to be open. Raup, however, cited evidence that no clearing had occurred since at least 1815. He further interpreted growth rings from tree stumps to show that the oldest trees had been released from competition as a consequence of the 1815 hurricane. Many of the younger trees had begun growing after that event, or had been saplings with suppressed growth until the 1815 hurricane also released them from competition. However, he found that for some large trees no release was evident in 1815. He interpreted this observation to mean that a certain amount of clearing had occurred prior to that date, because trees in cleared areas would show no release effect. He similarly concluded that the site was not truly virgin, but had been disturbed, although not so profoundly as to alter its tree composition.

As I consider their conclusions today, I find that Nichols and Raup had preconceived notions, which obscured for them the nature of coastal forests. The underlying assumption for their analyses was that a virgin system is one in which disturbance has not occurred. However, even though Raup hinted that the landscape was a dynamic one, he did not grasp fully his own words.

Shoreline forests are shaped by their physical environment. Coastal storms are frequent, and periodic damage from wind, storm surge, and wind-driven salt spray is considerable. Moreover, about once each century a storm creates catastrophic damage to these systems. In short, disturbance is a characteristic component of coastal systems. Coastal forests do not reach a steady state, but instead are dynamic and exhibit rather cyclic fluctuations in character.

By 2002, I had not been to the old forest in Stonington since my first visit 26 years earlier. I was studying the distribution of forest birds in Southeastern Connecticut that winter, and took the opportunity to drive past the area. I noted that nearly as long had passed since my last visit as had passed from the time of the 1938 hurricane to my first visit. As I stood on the road and looked into the leafless woodland, I could see that the even-aged stand of young trees had thinned. It had evolved into a maturing forest with most trees now over 60 years old, although scattered larger trees still punctuated the area. The forest's composition remained virtually identical to that reported by Nichols 90 years earlier, and by the earliest explorers 200 years before him. The canopy remained one of White Oak, Black Oak, Red Maple, Sassafras, and hickories, and the understory was predominantly Huckleberry.

I realized during my visit that I had now lived long enough to verify that this system is indeed one in dynamic equilibrium. That is, periodic and occasionally catastrophic changes shape its structure and composition. It grows trees, storms open the canopy, saplings are released from competition, and a new crop grows to replace those lost. Some of the previous generation survives, and provides a seed source for forest regeneration. Oaks in particular are favored because they regenerate well in forest openings caused by storms. In fact, there is no need to invoke clearing to explain the periodic openness of coastal forest.

So what are virgin conditions in an environment in which there is no undisturbed state? In my estimation, it is the state of this site as it exists to this day, and as it has existed for centuries.

FIELD TRIP
Barn Island Wildlife Management Area, Stonington

Directions: Barn Island may be reached by traveling east on U.S. Route 1 to Wequetequock. Look for a small sign pointing to Barn Island. Turn right onto Greenhaven Road, and then in a very short distance go right onto Palmer Neck Road. Follow this road to just before it ends in a parking lot and boat launch. A metal gate on the left marks the beginning of a wide trail that leads into the forest and adjacent tidal marsh. Follow this trail, and if you wish take some of the side trails to explore the interior forest further.

Equipment: Long pants, socks, a hat and insect repellent are essential for visiting this habitat, particularly during tick and mosquito season. Binoculars and field guides are also useful. If you wish to look over the tidal wetlands, a spotting scope is also most useful.

The habitat: Barn Island has fine examples of coastal forest. The area resembles closely the old Stonington forest in both its composition and structure. White Oak (*Quercus alba*), Black Oak (*Q. velutina*) and Mockernut Hickory (*Carya tomentosa*) are among the most characteristic tree species of this forest. All three are easy to distinguish. White Oak especially in winter appears to have flaky, whitish bark. In summer its round-lobed leaves characterize it. Black Oak, in contrast, has blocky, nearly black bark and pointed lobes on its leaves. Mockernut Hickory has aromatic compound (multi-part) leaves composed of 7-9 sharp-pointed, downy leaflets.

Smooth Holly

Other common forest species include Red Maple (*Acer rubrum*), Sassafras (*Sassafras albidum*), Black Cherry (*Prunus serotina*) and Black Birch (*Betula lenta*). In moister locations, Black Tupelo (*Nyssa sylvatica*) becomes common as well. In the understory, Huckleberry (*Gaylussacia baccata*) is common in drier spots, whereas Sweet Pepperbush (*Clethra alnifolia*), Spicebush (*Lindera benzoin*) Highbush Blueberry (*Vaccinium corymbosum*) and Winterberry (*Ilex verticillata*) are common in moister areas. Another pervasive feature of this forest is dense cover by vines, particularly the thorny, round-leaved Greenbriar (*Smilax rotundifolia*).

Straggling in from southern Rhode Island, where it is locally common, is the small tree American Holly (*Ilex opaca*). It is easiest to pick out from other forest trees in winter, because it retains its curious, spiny leaves year round. Another low, shrubby species, Smooth Holly (*I. glabra*), similarly straggles in from Rhode Island. It is also evergreen, but has oval, dark green leaves. Both hollies are widespread species of the coastal plain (sandy coastal lowlands found from southern New Jersey south), although both range north along the coast through northern New England. Strangely enough, American Holly is also a common forest tree of the southern Appalachians, where it grows nearly to the high elevation spruce-fir zone. Both species are present as well on Long Island, and I have presumed that their distribution in southeastern Connecticut is an artifact of that time in the geologic past when eastern Long Island was connected to Rhode Island. The present natural distribution of both species in Connecticut is somewhat problematic, however, as they are popular ornamentals that may escape from cultivation.

Wildlife: One of the more typical amphibians of the coastal zone is the Fowler's Toad. It is not restricted to this region, but it is specialized for the sandy, dry habitats that are frequent along the coast. Recessional moraines (sand and gravel left by retreating ice during glacial times) present near the coast are in part responsible for making such conditions common there. Another possible inhabitant of the Barn Island area is the Eastern Spadefoot. It occurs rarely and locally, but, like the hollies, it is a widespread species of the coastal plain and likely colonized southeastern Massachusetts, southeastern Connecticut and Rhode Island during that time when Long Island was connected to Rhode Island.

Reptiles of the Barn Island area include the Box Turtle, which like the two amphibians is associated frequently with dry, sandy

Fowler's Toad

areas. Similarly, the Eastern Hognose Snake is a typical species of these types of habitats. Another notable species of the region is the Black Rat Snake, a large, forest-dwelling snake that in Connecticut is distributed principally in southern Connecticut and the Connecticut River Valley.

Bird life of coastal forests has distinctive elements as well. The American Redstart presently reaches its greatest eastern Connecticut density in these forests. The species prefers more open and younger forests, and as regional forests have matured it has undergone local declines. Because coastal forests are frequently more open in character, it remains a comparatively common coastal species.

Another species once common in southeastern Connecticut but now largely extirpated from it is the Northern Parula. Local populations used the Beard Moss lichen (*Usnea*) as a nesting material almost exclusively. The lichen once hung in sheets from trees in coastal forests and swamps, although it largely disappeared from southern New England by the mid-20th century. Lichens as a group show sensitivity to air pollution, and this species appeared particularly susceptible to the effects of an industrializing landscape.

With the demise of Beard Moss, the Northern Parula disappeared. That is, almost disappeared. In a swampy coastal forest east of Barn Island I found in the summer of 2003 trees still festooned with Beard Moss. In this location I also found several territorial Northern Parulas, the first I have found in decades of exploring our region.

Still another notable feature of coastal forests that I discovered while performing year-round forest bird surveys is that in winter these forests fill with large numbers of our characteristic permanent residents. Birds like the Black-capped Chickadee, Tufted Titmouse and Downy Woodpecker build to numbers in winter greater than those of summer. Migration of birds from northern regions, as well as recruitment of juveniles from the local breeding population likely swell winter numbers.

Once upon a time, there was a species of mammal called the Sea Mink that may have plied the waters off of Barn Island. It is long extinct, however, and little is known of it. The Harbor Seal may still be seen in Little Narragansett Bay off Barn Island, but obviously neither of these species may be considered part of the coastal forest fauna. Typical species of the forest are the same as in any regional woodland: White-footed Mouse, Short-tailed Shrew, Southern Flying Squirrel, Gray Squirrel, Eastern Chipmunk. One of my only sightings of a Long-tailed Weasel occurred in coastal forest, but the species is not restricted to such habitats.

Closing thoughts: With the overwhelming development that has occurred all along the Connecticut shoreline, comparatively little remains of its natural landscape. Early reports suggest that areas of Pitch Pine (*Pinus rigida*) forest once occurred in some of the dry soils present near the coast. A small sample of this type of habitat is still present at Barn Island and at Rocky Neck State Park in East Lyme.

Another poorly represented habitat is coastal scrub. Fine examples exist at Barn Island and at Bluff Point State Park in

Groton, where scrubby areas occupy the seaward bluffs and edges of salt marshes. Characteristic shrubs and small trees include Beach Plum (*Prunus maritima*), High Tide Bush (*Iva frutescens*), Bayberry (*Myrica pensylvanicum*) and Groundsel Tree (*Baccharis halmifolia*).

Still other examples of scrub may be found at the seaward edge of Rocky Neck State Park and Hammonasset State Park in Clinton-Madison. Scrubby oaks like Scrub (*Quercus ilicifolia*) and Post Oak (*Q. stellata*) occur at these spots. Especially the latter two are typical understory shrubs of the coastal plain. As they approach their range limit, they are particularly prominent in (although not restricted to) coastal New England. A similar progression of coastal plain oak species occurs all along the East coast. To our south in New Jersey, the typically southeastern species, Southern Red (*Q. falcata*) and Willow Oak (*Q. phellos*), are similarly confined at their northern range limit to coastal environments.

One last example of a southern tree present in Connecticut is the Persimmon (*Diospyros virginiana*), which is common in coastal plain forests to the south, but which is historically known at this, its northern range limit, only from Lighthouse Point Park, New Haven. In the 1970s I observed a grove of these trees at the park, but they were faring poorly even then.

Riparian Habitats 12

Late one night while gathering information from John Hall Sage's collection catalog, I found tucked among the pages a card with notes penciled on its back. The book containing the card, as well as other aging volumes, was stored in the collections room at the University of Connecticut. I had come to like working alone in the overfilled, nearly windowless room, packed with specimens once living, but long since otherwise. Save for the passage of an occasional cockroach, it was a place where nothing interrupted my train of thought. So I sat that night nestled among the bones, my head swimming from the odor of mothballs, absently turning over the card to view its other side.

I expected that the pages of Sage's volume had rarely if ever been opened since he made his last entry in it. Before being rescued by the University it had sat for decades along with his collection, forgotten in the basement of Hartford's Wadsworth

Athenaeum. And in any event, the book did not make for riveting reading. It was a catalog in which he listed the bird specimens he had collected, along with information about their, sex, age and collection locality. He gave each a unique collection number, which corresponded to numbers attached to the specimens themselves. It was a compilation unusual for its era in the meticulousness of its entries and in its extended record of collection dates and locations. I used it as a key reference in drawing inferences about the historic distributions and populations of bird species in Connecticut. I still have my stacks of notes extracted from hours spent in front of his catalog.

As productive as my perusals through Sage's catalog might have been, I began to find it unsettling to look at page after page of his handwritten entries. They were a personal record, and not at all like the reams of perfectly printed pages that would characterize the records of a modern museum. I could see his handwriting evolve, as dates flowed from the 1870s, when the catalog began, to its end in the 1930s. I observed the passage of different pens, the steady compilation of a lifetime of knowledge, all now lost save for the entries on those pages. The book carried on a dialogue with me across time in the words of its author, and now I touched those same pages once touched by him, that likely still contained imbedded within them his very molecules. The catalog itself was a specimen, of one once living, but now otherwise.

It wasn't that he recorded anything private in those entries. They were all matter-of-fact lists, rather like an old-fashioned bank ledger, which was not surprising as Sage was a banker. Science was an avocation with him, not a profession. But then there was the card. I turned it over. He had penciled his note on a copy of his daughter's wedding invitation, doubtless one left over after the event itself had occurred. The exact date is lost to my memory, but it was some time around 1912. My father was being born; Sage's daughter was being married. I was crushed. On our perceived

Floodplain forest, Portland

continuous thread of time, all that separated John Hall Sage from me was a series of instants well within living memory. I realized how much I wanted to know this person, yet no matter how badly I might wish it I could not.

I thought about contacting his daughter, as she might still be alive, although I did not. I did visit the historical society in Portland, where he lived, where I talked to an elderly woman who had known him. I visited his personal library, now at Trinity College in Hartford. I drove past his house, again and again. But he was not home, nor would he be. There was nothing more I could do but again confront the limitations of mortality.

The woman at the Portland historical society had shown me a pamphlet that Sage had written listing the birds found in his yard. I wondered if it was the only copy left in existence. Much of what I read was rather like what I knew from the vicinity. I had been working in the riparian habitats of Portland and neighboring Cromwell for a year gathering data for a master's thesis, and already knew the area well. In his catalog, Sage primarily mentioned local places, particularly the Little River marshes (now called Cromwell Meadows), Gildersleeve Island, and Wangunk Meadows. All three were principal study sites of mine.

Sage had been exploring these sites less than 40 years before I began, and now I have been studying the same places for 30 years. Although the surrounding countryside has overwhelmingly suburbanized, during my visits the areas themselves have hardly changed. I have even mapped vegetation patterns in them over this time, which show remarkably little alteration. Many of the trees present in the sites are so old that they must appear much the same as when Sage looked at them. It is one of the features I like especially about mature natural areas. Their constancy in an increasingly vinyl and asphalt landscape is a comfort. The effects of time slow to a level that permits one to gain from them a sense of stability.

I have just returned from my millionth or so visit to Wangunk Meadows in Portland. It was discouraging to see the new housing developments on the opposite shore of the Connecticut River, in areas I long remember as fine lowland forest. But the meadows themselves have remained constant. I first visited them on a leafless, cold March day, much like this icy November morning nearly 30 years later, and as I explored about, that first day was still clear in my mind. All the same pleasure and fascination remained, much as I imagine it did for John Sage. It is a good place for a field trip.

Field Trip
Wangunk Meadows Wildlife Mgmt. Area, Portland

Directions: From Route 66, take Route 17 north about 4.5 miles across the Portland town line into Glastonbury. Turn left on Old Maid's Lane, past what was recently farmland although it now grows houses. Follow it to the end, and turn left on Tryon St., which borders the Connecticut River. In about 400 yards a parking area for Wangunk Meadows will appear on the left, just before a locked gate.

Equipment: At least rubber boots are useful in this generally wet area. To view well the wetlands, hip boots are a better choice. Mosquitoes and ticks are abundant at certain times of year, so long pants, socks, long sleeve shirts, hats and insect repellent are wise choices. Binoculars and field guides are also helpful for appreciating the area. During the hunting season, the area should be avoided during peak hunting hours (early morning and late afternoon). I recommend that orange reflective clothing be worn during this season.

The habitat: The trip along Route 17 may be considered part of this expedition. Along a good part of its length, the road straddles the dividing line between the gray metamorphic rocks of the eastern Connecticut hills and the red sandstones of the Connecticut Valley. It then ascends along the edge of the hills and looks down on the eastern edge of the valley. The view is best observed when trees are without leaves.

The meadows themselves are firmly within the Connecticut Valley. Their configuration superficially appears to be a consequence of a time when the channel of the Connecticut River flowed through the area. Such instability in the courses of rivers flowing through flat valleys is typical, and gave rise to such features as the Connecticut River oxbow at Northampton, Massachusetts. The oxbow was made famous by the early 19th century painting of Thomas Cole. Cole's painting is, in fact, a valuable if somewhat romanticized view of how the Connecticut Valley appeared before the era of photography. However, the site has a more complex origin. Retreating ice from glacial times paused along the southern margin of Wangunk Meadows, and debris in glacial meltwater formed a delta upon which Wangunk Meadows later developed.

The first view to greet the visitor to Wangunk Meadows remains strikingly like that of Cole's interpretation. The pastoral farmland of 19th century New England survives, as do massive trunks of ancient trees. The river itself is a placid vision, and in the quiet light of early morning, before the motorboats and chainsaws awake, it is still one of peaceful continuity. Some of Connecticut's landscapes may appear disappointing when compared with those of other regions, but those of the Connecticut River are exceptional.

As they have since their inception, the riparian areas of

Wangunk Meadows, as well as those of other floodplain zones of the Connecticut River, play several key ecological roles. These regions are called floodplains because they are the receptacles for floodwaters. Floods may occur after major storms, but they occur particularly in early spring when snowmelt swells rivers to overflowing. Floodwaters carry with them minerals and dissolved nutrients, and such nutrients make the areas fertile. Much of southern New England's remaining farmland persists on the fertile and renewing soils of floodplains. Moreover, by accepting floodwaters, these areas function in natural flood protection. They are areas in which construction is a poor idea, as it is in their natural state that they perform their most valuable human services.

The first natural riparian habitat encountered at Wangunk Meadows is well-developed floodplain forest. It exhibits much of the classically described structure of the floodplain. Depending on the energy associated with the flooding water, soils develop that support differing floras. The highest energy environments are found along the riverbank, where swifter water deposits sandier sediments. Such sediments can pile up into a levee. These levee environments are moist but comparatively well drained.

An unusual variety of tree species establish themselves on the levee and riverbank, many of which are associated primarily with the floodplain environment. Species like the American Elm (*Ulmus americana*), Slippery Elm (*U. rubra*), Silver Maple (*Acer saccharinum*), Eastern Cottonwood (*Populus deltoides*) and American Sycamore (*Platanus occidentalis*) are among these. The latter three species attain among the greatest sizes of any trees in Connecticut. Monumental specimens of each may be seen in the Wangunk Meadows area. More widespread species that join them on the levee include the American Linden (*Tilia americana*), Red Maple (*A. rubrum*), White Ash (*Fraxinus americana*), Bitternut Hickory (*Carya cordiformis*) and Shagbark Hickory (*C. ovata*).

A species I have not encountered in the Portland area although

I have found it further north on the Connecticut River is River Birch (*Betula nigra*), a tree frequently cultivated for its striking salmon pink, peeling bark. Another attractive species with star-shaped leaves is the Sweetgum (*Liquidambar styraciflua*). It is characteristic of floodplains further south, but native with us only in extreme southwestern Connecticut. Elsewhere in the state it is planted as an ornamental. In much of its range it forms a characteristic floodplain community called Sweetgum-Pin Oak forest, extensive examples of which occur in similarly glacial-derived wetlands as close to us as northeastern New Jersey.

Further away from the river behind the levee, a lower lying area sometimes called the flat develops. It is characterized by finer soils that can be carried further from the river by the decreasing energy of floodwaters. It develops a layer beneath its surface called a hard pan, a dense layer impervious to percolation by water. Hence, the soils of the flat are frequently waterlogged and with low oxygen. Ponding of water often occurs on the surface of the flat. In these more extreme conditions where trees may have to endure weeks of inundation, certain species predominate. Silver Maple is again abundant, and it is joined there by Red Maple (*A. rubrum*), Pin Oak (*Quercus palustris*), Swamp White Oak (*Q. bicolor*), Slippery Elm and American Elm. White Ash is largely replaced by a species more tolerant of flooding, the Green Ash (*F. pennsylvanica*).

The understory of floodplain forests is often poorly represented in part as a consequence of mechanical damage to shrubs during flooding. However, certain species may be found, including the small tree Boxelder (*Acer negundo*), and the shrubs Winterberry (*Ilex verticillata*), Common Elder (*Sambucus canadensis*), Highbush Blueberry (*Vaccinium corymbosum*), Spicebush (*Lindera benzoin*) and Arrowwood (*Viburnum recognitum*). Riverbank Grape (*Vitis riparia*), Poison Ivy (*Toxicodendron radicans*) and other vines species may densely cover certain areas, particularly those where forest openings occur.

The herbaceous component of floodplain forest is often characterized by dense stands of single species. Sensitive Fern (*Onoclea sensibilis*) and Cinnamon Fern (*Osmunda cinnamomea*) typically do this, as does Reed Canary Grass (*Phalaris arundinacea*). Another notable species of the Connecticut River floodplain is the Ostrich Fern (*Matteucia struthiopteris*), which has giant fronds (leaves) shaped like ostrich plumes. All three of

Cinnamon fern

these fern species have separate vegetative and reproductive fronds. As ferns are primitive plants, they reproduce by means of spores, and the reproductive fronds shed these spores at maturity. The spore-bearing fronds look rather like variations on a theme of cinnamon sticks. Other characteristic floodplain herbs include Lady Fern (*Athyrium filix-femina*), Royal Fern (*Osmunda regalis*), Clearweed (*Pilea pumula*), False Nettle (*Boehmeria cylindrica*), and a variety of attractive grasses, including White Grass (*Leersia virginica*) and Wood Reed (*Cinna arundinacea*).

One of the great attractions of Wangunk Meadows is that floodplain forest is only one of two major riparian habitats present. The other, riverine marsh, is a considerably less common habitat. It is distinctive among Connecticut River marshes in being a non-tidal, deep water system over much of its extent. The plant communities develop in water 1-3 feet deep, and are characterized by species like Tuckahoe (*Peltandra virginica*), Bullhead Lily (*Nuphar variegatum*), Bur-reed (*Sparganium eurycarpum*), Smartweed (*Polygonum* spp.; at least three species), Water-dock

(*Rumex verticillatus*) and Manna Grass (*Glyceria acutifolia*). In shallower areas, species like the primitive spore-bearing Water Horsetail (*Equisetum fluviatile*) is common, along with River Bulrush (*Scirpus fluviatilis*), Calamus (*Acorus calamus*), Blue Flag (*Iris versicolor*) and Reed Canary Grass. In late summer, much of the area grows up to Wild Rice (*Zizania aquatica*). Forming an interface between the marsh and forest is still another habitat, shrub swamp, where species like Buttonball Bush (*Cephalanthus occidentalis*), Speckled Alder (*Alnus rugosa*) and Red Osier Dogwood (*Cornus amomum*) occur.

Wildlife: Occurring at Wangunk Meadows along with the ubiquitous Connecticut pond frogs (Green Frog, Bullfrog, Pickerel Frog) is a species of limited local distribution, the Northern Leopard Frog. In Connecticut it occurs primarily in the Central Valley and northwestern part of the state. It is common in all Connecticut River marshes I have visited.

A variety of turtle species also may be found in these riparian habitats. A characteristic one of floodplain forest is the Wood Turtle. In deeper water portions of marshes, the Eastern Painted Turtle and Snapping Turtle are common, although the Spotted and Musk Turtle also can inhabit muddy and marshy environments.

Wood Turtle

Typical marsh snakes are the Northern Water and Eastern Ribbon Snake.

The premier inhabitants of Wangunk Meadows are the birds. A diverse assemblage occurs in riparian habitats, including a number of Connecticut's most notable species. Birds were Sage's principal attraction to the area, as well as my own. Among the few places I have found summering American Bitterns in Connecticut are the marshes of the Portland area, including Wangunk Meadows. Sage similarly found them in Portland, although he too considered them rare breeders. Wangunk Meadows is also one of the few places I have seen summering Northern Harriers, although in Sage's day they were a fairly common breeder in the still agricultural landscapes of Connecticut.

Another species largely absent from Connecticut as a breeder is the Sora, although I have found it summering at all three major Portland area marshes. It is an extremely secretive member of the rail family, best detected by its distinctive call. Even in this regard it is difficult to locate because it has only a brief season (primarily mid- to late May) for calling. The deep, non-tidal waters of Wangunk Meadows appear to be particularly good habitat for it, as I have found it there consistently. Sage also found nesting birds in Portland, but similarly considered the species a rare breeder. Few individuals spent more time exploring marshes than Sage, so his perspective on this enigmatic species is a valuable historical one.

I now have historical observations of my own. On June 3, 1974, I found the nest of a Black Duck in grass bordering one of the tongues of marsh in the Wangunk Meadows system, a species that at the time I considered fairly common. I could not have known it then, but it would be the last such nest I would find away from the salt marshes of the lower Connecticut River. In fact, during the period 1974 to 1994, I documented the virtual extirpation of the Black Duck from freshwater portions of the river. This decline was part of a larger one occurring throughout much of the species' range. Sage also thought the Black Duck was a rare breeder, although he wrote during the height of the market-gunning era, when unregulated hunting had drastically reduced many of the continent's game bird populations.

In addition to the marshes, the adjacent shrub swamps are populated by their own characteristic species. The Willow

Flycatcher, Yellow Warbler, Common Yellowthroat and Song Sparrow are all members of this fauna. Moreover, the floodplain forest is alive with birds, although its open understory reduces the number of ground-nesting species present in it. Species present are frequently those associated with forest openings, which are created by the juxtaposition of forest and marsh and mechanical damage by flooding. Characteristic community members include the Red-shouldered Hawk, Black-billed Cuckoo, Yellow-throated Vireo, Warbling Vireo, Baltimore Oriole, Orchard Oriole, American Redstart, Indigo Bunting and Rose-breasted Grosbeak. In addition, I once found in a forest opening grown up to tangled vines and shrubs a Yellow-breasted Chat, a common southern species, but one very infrequent with us. Chats were very common in the open landscapes of Sage's day, but they have since disappeared from our area along with farms and early successional brush.

A distinctive assemblage of aquatic and semi-aquatic mammals is found along major floodplains, and is present in the Portland area. Muskrats are common especially where there are marshes. Their larger cousin, the Beaver, also occurs in these areas. Weasel relatives present include the Mink and River Otter. In the grassy borders of marshes, Meadow Jumping Mice and Meadow Voles may be found. In adjacent floodplain forest, White-footed Mice and Red-backed Voles are to be expected, although I suspect their densities are lower than in forests not periodically inundated. An interesting project might be to study the population dynamics of small mammals in floodplain habitats.

Closing thoughts: There are several other examples of riparian systems with public access. A pastoral spot within sight of downtown Hartford is Wethersfield Meadows. Although the area is in private ownership, public dirt roads traverse an area that includes extensive farmland, floodplain forest, and an exceptional riverine marsh. Moreover, Folley Brook Preserve is at the north end of Wethersfield bordering Wethersfield Cove, and Riverside Park is within the city limits of Hartford.

Directly across the river in Cromwell is Cromwell Fish and Wildlife Management Area, John Sage's favorite collecting location. It will be the topic of a separate field trip. In it, there are vast areas of River Bulrush-dominated marsh, along with a variety of other marsh communities and floodplain forest. However, much of the area is now surrounded by interstate highway, industry and shopping plazas, and its sediments are contaminated with an industrial cocktail of poisons. At one end a now closed landfill has gobbled up a significant swath of former marsh. In addition, at some point in the past attempts at "improving" the marsh for waterfowl resulted in channels being carved through a large section of it. Although there is still much that remains photogenic in this extensive system, it is just as well that Sage cannot see his Little River marshes in this sorry state.

Tidal Marshes 13

It has been several years since I last set foot on Great Island, a large tidal marsh at the mouth of the Connecticut River. However, I expect I will visit again, as there is on it a place I want to see once more. During one of my earlier trips I chanced upon the initials J.N.C. carved into a rock. Chiseled as they were with 19th century script, I knew instinctively that they were those of John N. Clark, a Saybrook judge who near this spot in 1876 found the first Black Rails on the Connecticut River.

John Clark lived so long ago that no living memory of him survives. His remains consist solely of a series of brief articles written in long extinct periodicals. I know him from only those printed words, but from the words I have developed some notion of who he was. It is a rather incomplete view, as I can learn little of his disposition from these articles. But still, it would appear we had many interests in common, and I have wondered if we would have been friends had we known each other.

Despite the silence that descends between beings separated by time, John Clark and I do share a bond. In 1987, after 14 years of trying, I finally found Black Rails in his Saybrook marshes. Over a 111 year interval only the two of us had found them. The marsh is different than it was in Judge Clark's day. It has been ditched for mosquito control, a landfill has destroyed part of its area, and it is now ringed with houses that were not yet present even when I began studies. However, the rails remain. I expect Judge Clark would be pleased.

Some future day I expect a dusty copy of this book will be found by some curious individual on a library shelf, in a manner similar to the way I found copies of John Clark's articles in the back rooms of old libraries. I expect also that some individual may wonder, as I have done, about its author. My chronicle below is in part intended to provide those clues for the future reader that I do not have, nor can I ever have, for John Clark.

Some of my acquaintances would consider me very quiet. However, were it possible for them to hear at wavelengths not available to ears, their view might alter. Could they hear the persistent din that I do, they might themselves long for silence. The issue is, and has always been, my mind. I cannot turn it off. It insists I pay attention; it wakes me from sound sleep. It insists further that I write. My mind works through the same thought repeatedly, forming and progressively polishing words until they finally reach the pen.

I do not consider myself a writer, yet I write compulsively and continually, on scraps of paper, on napkins, at breakfast, in the bathroom; most any time that several instants avail themselves to me. I do not lie in bed at night reading, but lie there writing. It is a necessary bodily function, like breathing. I also breathe every day; yet similarly I do not define myself as a breather.

But writing for me is a private act. I rarely allow anyone to

know the words I write. They are private. They are my personal dealings with the ephemeral state called life. However, I have saved some of my assorted papers, and as I prepared this chapter I knew there were certain of them I wished at last to share.

The topic is tidal marshes. I came to Connecticut in 1973 with the idea that I would study birds of tidal marshes. I did so, and continued observing them intermittently from 1974 to 2000. I may yet do more. Some time before the era of my Black Rail discoveries, on a hot July morning that is now itself a long time ago, I began writing a series of paragraphs on the backs of muddy envelopes while carrying out those studies. I was researching by canoe the tidal marshes at the mouth of the Connecticut River at a place called Great Island:

3:30 AM: Before me lies Great Island, brooding in the star shine of its millionth night on Earth. It is a maze of creeks and mud and salt meadows, situated at the place where the river is swallowed into the sea. It is a place known best to non-human creatures, for on it they have left their bones in an unbroken lineage extending to the day of its birth.

My rowing takes me along the shoreline, such as it is, with grasses emerging directly from the water and from sod clumps strewn along the water's edge. I search for a landmark, an indentation in the line of grass, until at last I find it: the creek that leads to the interior. The creek is narrow, and low tide makes the route cavernous, an effect intensified by the ragged canopy of grass extending above on both sides. With effort, I pole to the shallowest water, seeking to penetrate as far into the island as the tide will allow.

Only when the mud refuses further progress do I stop and strain to listen. In Audubon's day an enigmatic bird called the Black Rail lived here, and it was said that it called only in the darkness of early morning on a moonless night. I have never found even a hint that it might be present.

4:15 AM: A solitary clatter arises from a distant stand of bulrushes. I look up to note the weakening blackness with hints of gray extending to the zenith. More clattering and bubbling soon follow. The Marsh Wrens have begun their day. Growled "quocks" from several Night Herons flapping overhead further break the stillness, and I also become aware that I have absently begun wiping my arms of the biting insects that have emerged. I endure the insects at first, but they ravage my face and arms, and soon drive me to open water.

I make my way back down the creek, occasionally glimpsing shadowy forms fluttering past or clinging to overhanging reeds. Marsh Wrens rise and float between perches and, with epaulettes flaring, Red-winged Blackbirds spar over ill-defined patches of ground. For an instant, a Least Bittern appears from the creek bank, but as quickly as it appears it vanishes among the bulrushes. Still another movement catches my eye: drooping bill, long toes curving inward as its leg lifts from the mud- a Clapper Rail. It turns and utters a soft "whirr." Then, with tail flicking, it climbs the bank and slips between adjacent stems into the marsh interior.

I stop my progress to assimilate what lies before me: a gray-green sheet, foul with sulfur, spangled in swollen dewdrops, and writhing in the exuberance of the approaching day.

5:30 AM: Light fog has begun rolling down the valley, and quiet returns when it seethes between the hills and muffles the frenzy accompanying first light. Bird activity has begun drifting toward silence as the sky dims to is pre-dawn state, but through the veil a *bleeding sun momentarily boils a hole, perching on the seed heads of last year's reeds before evaporating back into the mist.*

I have been rowing fiercely to reach another spot before morning advances too far, and the day's first beads of perspiration have begun to form on my brow. Although mist continues to cool the air, I begin to fear that another humid summer morning has begun to build to a scorching crescendo. Moving upriver, I note that salt meadow is becoming confined to tongues and patches among the increasingly extensive stands of reeds and cattails. The effect of seawater is diminishing.

I wipe the condensation from my binoculars and scan the approaching mudflats. A concentration of Black Ducks dabbles in the channel, and a lingering yellowlegs repeatedly probes into the shallows of a tide pool, seeming to sense in its urgency the waning low tide and impending loss of feeding grounds. I also just glimpse a hen Gadwall leading her brood into a bordering stand of grasses.

The morning is racing. Another creek exits near the mudflat, and I decide to explore it before the final vestiges of morning coolness are lost. I head toward it, and upon entering I am engulfed by walls of reeds that extend along both banks. Lacing the canopy are strands of webs left by spiders that somehow managed to span the banks. They are strung with beads of dew, and both they and the overhanging reeds drip in the thickening fog. I struggle up the channel, peering above at the slit of sky where swallows dart past, continuing until I can go no further.

7:00 AM: I tie my canoe to a clump of reeds and, grasping handfuls of stems, pull myself onto the bank. From here I plan to reach a wooded outcrop that dominates north end of the island. It is impossible to see far enough to gain a bearing, so I set my compass and begin to push through the reeds, hoisting myself over piles of dead stems and forcing my legs through the splintering brown stalks.

Looking about me I see that the trail I have blazed has evaporated, and that nothing is visible save for the reeds about me. My back has *begun to fill with leaf sheaths and disintegrating seed heads, and broken stems slip down my clothes, catching at my knees and stabbing my ankles. Sweat now trickles down my stomach, where it makes the bits of debris collecting around my waist sting. I have reached a spot where I must follow a creek upstream because incoming tidewater has made it too deep to ford. Continuing on I find a narrow spot, so I take a chance and jump across. As I do I am tugged from behind by attached stems, and my feet slide from beneath me on the algae coating the bank. But finally I push forward through rows of reed, and shaking myself I see a patch of salt meadow before me. Not more than 50 yards beyond is the outcrop.*

9:00 AM: I climb over briars that ring the outcrop. Several Ospreys fly past with fish grasped in their talons. One nest sits nearby in the sun-bleached skeleton of a dead oak, and still another nestles on the ground among driftwood. Already, however, bird activity is predominantly the province of the gulls, a string of whom fly by chasing another with a scrap of food in its bill. Otherwise calling is intermittent, and few birds are still about actively feeding.

The rising heat drives the fog above the trees, and shafts of light penetrate the disintegrating clouds to fully illuminate a silver, shimmering scene that dazzles me to forgetfulness. I do not know how long I stare. It is too beautiful to look away.

Field Trip
Great Island Wildlife Management Area, Old Lyme

Directions: Take Rt. 156 south into Old Lyme. Cross under the junction of Interstate 95, and continue south until Smith's Neck Road appears on the right. Take this road to its end, where there is a boat launch and parking lot. Opposite the boat launch is Great Island.

Equipment: This expedition will be a bit more daring than some of the trips in this book, although it is still well within the means of most individuals to accomplish. There are some dangers to exploring tidal marshes (I have sunk to my waist in the mud of tidal creeks on an incoming tide, and almost not been able to extract myself), but by following the suggestions below a visit can be kept safe.

For the non-adventurous, hats, long pants, insect repellent, binoculars and field guides are recommended. Observations can be made directly from the boat launch. For the more adventurous, canoes can be used to explore the interior of the island. It is a short trip to the island across a quiet creek. Access is best at high tide, when canoes may be taken into the island's tidal creeks. While exploring, it is safest to remain in the canoe, and in any event observing is generally best from a canoe. However, the marsh surface may be traversed on foot (I recommend hip boots to anyone wishing to walk on the marsh), although there are certain risks in doing so. Wading across tidal creeks is risky, and it is easy to fall into mosquito control ditches or soft spots on the marsh surface. In late summer especially, care should be taken to avoid mosquito bites and mosquito-borne diseases. Particularly in cooler weather, precautions should be taken to avoid tick bites. Also in summer, the vicinity of Osprey nests should be avoided so that nesting birds are not disturbed. Ospreys may be aggressive near nests.

The habitat: The lower Connecticut River is an estuary, a place where river water mixes with seawater and is affected by tides. Great Island is situated at the mouth of the river, and is perhaps the most superb example in Connecticut of an estuarine tidal marsh. Such tidal marshes are truly critical ecological systems within the coastal landscape. They are notable, for example, for their high productivity (the rate of manufacture of living material), which is among the highest of temperate systems. This productivity is a consequence in large part of tidal action, which brings nutrients and minerals to the marsh, aerates the marsh's surface, and flushes away wastes.

Most of the prodigious production of the marsh is not actually consumed directly, but enters the estuarine system as detritus, or

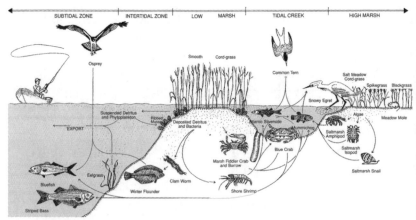

Reprinted from Tidal Marshes of Long Island Sound. Courtesy Connecticut College Arboretum

dead plant remains. Plant detritus is one of the key components of fuel for the estuary, and provides energy to power microorganism and ultimately animal productivity. The creeks of tidal wetlands are well known, for example, as a key nursery ground for a number of important game fish.

The ecological characteristics of tidal wetlands also have been associated with an ability to cleanse water of excess nutrients supplied by such human activities as sewage production. The wetlands' capacity to produce make them capable of converting excess nutrients into biological productivity. Moreover, the low energy environments of these wetlands act to filter fine sediments from water, thereby improving water clarity.

As the concentration of salt in the water diminishes away from the river mouth, a succession of plant associations appears that ranges from cordgrass at the island's seaward end to cattail and reed dominated communities at its upriver end. Also present at the southernmost tip of Great Island are the vestiges of Poverty Island, which in the 19th century was a separate sandy island at the river mouth. This beach-like area is vegetated by Dune Grass (*Ammophila breviligulata*), Seaside Goldenrod (*Solidago sempervirens*) and High Tide Bush (*Iva frutescens*).

The south end of Great Island has the most extensive examples of salt marsh habitat. Salt marsh is an environment characterized by plant and animal species that tolerate tidal inundation with saline water. Stands of Salt Marsh Cordgrass (*Spartina alterniflora*; in the grass family, *Gramineae*) occur in that portion of the marsh referred to as low marsh: that region from approximately mid-tide to mean high tide. It is thus found along tidal creeks and at lower microelevations. Particularly further upriver where water salinity begins to diminish, other species of cordgrass also appear, including *S. pectinata* and, less commonly, *S. cynosuroides*. These two handsome species are best located in mid-late summer when their seed heads are fully mature. One last species commonly found in this zone and occasionally predominating in it is Salt Marsh Bulrush (*Scirpus robustus*; in the sedge family).

Above this level in less frequently flooded locations is that region called high marsh. Salt Meadow Cordgrass (*S. patens*) dominates this region, and co-occurs with species like Salt Grass (*Distichlis spicata*). Other notable salt marsh specialists include Seaside Arrow-grass (*Triglochin maritima*), Salt Marsh Aster (*Aster tenuifolius*), Seaside Gerardia (*Gerardia maritima*) and Sea Lavender (*Limonium nashii*).

At greater microelevations on Great Island, and toward the upland edge of many tidal marshes, Salt Meadow Cordgrass gives way to Black Grass (*Juncus gerardi*; in the rush family, *Juncaceae*). When contrasted with the pale green tussocks of Salt Meadow Cordgrass, Black Grass indeed appears black. At still higher microelevations, Switchgrass (*Panicum virgatum*), Rose Mallow (*Hibiscus palustris*) and several shrubby species like High Tide Bush come to predominate. At tidal marshes that merge into uplands, species like these form the boundary vegetation between marsh and upland.

Other notable environments in the salt marsh are salt pannes. At high tide, these surface depressions can become filled with water that does not easily drain away. As the sun evaporates their water, pannes become increasingly saline. In this "hypersaline" environment, only a handful of specialized species occur. A stunted form of Salt Marsh Cordgrass occurs, as does the fleshy-stemmed Saltwort (*Salicornia* spp.). The aquatic plant Widgeon Grass (*Ruppia maritima*; in the pondweed family, *Najadaceae*) may occur as well.

King Rail nest

Salt marsh is replaced by plant communities of brackish (slightly saline) water at the upriver end of Great Island. Switchgrass becomes fairly common at some spots, although Narrow-leaved Cattail (*Typha angustifolia*) and Reed (*Phragmites communis*) are the most widespread species. However, photo stations I first established in 1974 have shown progressive changes in the vegetation of this portion of the island. Patches of salt marsh have become less widespread, apparently at least in part because of lunar cycles that influence the degree to which salt water intrudes upriver. In addition, places that were primarily Narrow-leaved Cattail in 1974 are now predominantly vegetated by Reed. Although Reed is a native Connecticut species, an aggressive alien form has become established that replaces cattails in brackish portions of the river.

Wildlife: The aquatic life of salt marshes is distinctive and characterized by species capable of surviving in both salt and fresh water, or of being inundated with water and exposed to air. At low tide, three species of Fiddler Crabs (*Uca pugnax, U. pugulator* and, less commonly, *U. minax*) come out of their burrows along tidal creeks to scavenge for food. The males are notable for their enlarged claw, which is used in courtship and combat rather than for feeding. They share the tidal creeks with species like the Green Crab (*Carcinus maenis*), Ribbed Mussel (*Geukensia demissa*) and Mud Snail (*Ilyanassa obsoleta*). Another snail that commonly attaches itself to stems of cordgrass is the Salt Marsh Snail (*Melampus bidentatus*).

In the tidal creek waters, juveniles of some of our important game fish may be found, including the Striped Bass (*Morone saxatilis*) and Bluefish (*Pomatomus saltatrix*). Common small fish species include the Mummichog (*Fundulus heteroclitus*), Four-spined Stickleback (*Apeltes quadracus*) and Atlantic Silversides (*Menida menida*). The creeks are also inhabited by our native shrimp, *Palaeomonetes pugio*.

Virtually no amphibians are found in salt marsh habitats, as they are poorly adapted to saline environments. I have occasionally collected Green, Bull and Pickerel Frogs at the upland border of salt marshes where freshwater streams enter, but otherwise they are absent. However, reptiles are another story. The brackish specialist Northern Diamondback Terrapin is fairly common in the larger tidal creeks of Great Island. Snapping Turtles also sometimes venture into the less saline waters of the island's north end. I have on occasion observed snakes in salt marshes as well, particularly the Black Racer and Northern Water Snake. Other species occurring along salt marsh borders include the Fowler's Toad, American Toad, Red-backed Salamander, Eastern Garter Snake and Eastern Hognose Snake.

Unlike the reptiles and amphibians, bird life of tidal marshes is distinctive and varied. The Seaside Sparrow, for example, is an abundant resident of tidal creeks and other areas of low marsh. It is replaced in high marsh by the also abundant Sharp-tailed Sparrow. These species are able to concentrate excess salt from their diet and eliminate it via their specialized kidneys. Where salt marsh is replaced by reeds and cattails, the Swamp Sparrow replaces both these species.

Rails are among the oddest of marsh birds. They fly rarely, and in fact behave more like mice than birds. They are best seen at low tide, when they slip out of the marsh vegetation onto the muddy borders of tidal creeks. The Clapper Rail, which concentrates excess dietary salt via a specialized salt gland, is

Tricolored Heron

fairly common and typical of salt marsh habitats. It is replaced by the smaller, redder Virginia Rail in cattail-reed areas. The King Rail, which is the size of the Clapper Rail but the color of the Virginia Rail, is a rare but regularly occurring species of more brackish areas. One other likely resident is the Black Rail, which I have found directly across the river at Ragged Rock Creek, but never on Great Island. The diminutive, gray Sora is principally a rail of freshwater marshes, but may be seen as a migrant at Great Island in fall (beginning as early as July).

Another notable species of the tidal marsh is the belligerent and amusing Marsh Wren. It builds domed nests that it attaches to adjacent stems of cattails or reeds. Many of the nests encountered are actually "dummy" nests, which males build to attract mates. Other easily observed species of tidal marshes include the herons, with the Snowy Egret being most commonly encountered. Moreover, the Glossy Ibis, Great Egret, Tricolored Heron, Black-crowned Night Heron and Yellow-crowned Night Heron also frequent tidal marsh creeks.

The most conspicuous bird of the tidal marsh is the loudly vocal Osprey, which now nests fairly commonly throughout Great Island. It may be observed diving into shallow water to capture fish, which are its principal prey. Although eastern Long Island Sound is historically an area of great breeding density for Ospreys, when I began studies in 1974 only a single infertile pair was present in the Connecticut River estuary. The species had declined to this low point as a consequence of environmental pollution with persistent pesticides and PCBs. Since then, it has begun to repopulate and expand its range along the river.

Comparatively few species of mammals inhabit tidal marshes. I have found that the Meadow Jumping Mouse and Meadow Vole are among the most abundant small species in the salt marsh. The Muskrat also is common, and the characteristic stick nest composed of cattail and reed stems may be found on Great Island. Some individuals build nests in the banks of tidal creeks, and others use tussocks of Salt Meadow Cordgrass for nesting. Additional species I have observed using salt marshes and their edges include the Red Fox, Striped Skunk, Long-tailed Weasel, Mink, Opossum and White-tailed Deer.

Closing thoughts: Entirely different types of tidal marshes exist along the Connecticut River. A short distance upriver in Lyme, freshwater tidal marshes make their first appearance. These habitats have a more diverse flora, and all the animals specialized for life in salt marshes disappear. Several distinctive plant associations occur in these marshes, although their character changes from spring to fall. Deeper water and tidal areas are dominated by Pickerelweed (*Pontederia cordata*) and Water Lotus (*Nuphar variegatum*) in early summer, but often grow up to Wild Rice (*Zizania aquatica*) by late summer. Other communities present include intergrading associations dominated by such species as River Bulrush (*Scirpus fluviatilis*), Calamus (*Acorus calamus*), Tuckahoe (*Peltandra virginica*), Tussock Sedge (*Carex stricta*) and the primitive, spore-bearing plant Water Horsetail (*Equisetum fluviatile*).

Freshwater Marshes 14

T*is a gift to be simple, a gift to be free* are the words of an ancient Shaker hymn. They are quintessential Yankee ideas, rooted in Puritanism, and formalized by Thoreau.

Simplicity. After marathon deliberations, my closest childhood friend and I concluded, as Thoreau had, that stripping away all non-essentials was crucial for confronting the nature of being. We experimented with stark and contemplative lifestyles. We went so far as to make extended journeys into wilderness, devoid of most everything material. How simple could we make it, and what would we learn by doing so?

Another friend and I debated freedom. If there were a choice to be made, as it appeared to us there often was, would it be better to choose freedom or security? I chose freedom, arguing that one could have a secure but pointless existence. In fact, I continued, most everyone I knew had a secure and pointless existence.

Although my friend liked my argument, she still chose security. Nor am I so certain she should have opted otherwise. A life of no security would also be a hard one. And this debate was not simply a hypothetical one. We were deciding how we would conduct our lives.

But how could one be free—free to explore being? I was skeptical that it could be among the world of humans. I believed, like Thoreau, that simplicity would be a key ingredient in that it would remove much of what clouded vision. I further expected that wildness apart from people would be the place to explore. In college I hatched an idea. Moses had sought wisdom on the mountain, Thoreau had sought it among the trees; I would seek it in the low and wet places.

I thought my choice was better. I would investigate marshes because they are simpler landscapes. They are two-dimensional. They have length and width; height in them is a nominal dimension. I reasoned that, just as the gravitational warping of space was most readily visualized by examining the effect of a mass on a two-dimensional rubber surface, the nature of existence might be more readily grasped in the two dimensions of a marsh. Even that fourth dimension, time, appeared as if it might have its effects diminished within at least certain types of marshes. In the words of Thoreau, "simplify, simplify." My college professors teased me about my notions of marshes. I would tell them that I could learn more of being from marsh birds than I could from people.

I decided the time to act had come, and the stage would be the Connecticut River. Along this river there were an extensive series of marshes that had been ignored by urban onslaught. They had purity unlike other places; they were virgin landscapes. Their ages could be measured in thousands of years, and in that time the hand of humanity on them had been nominal. But they were awful and difficult places. People rarely ventured to their interior. I could escape from humanness there. Better yet, I knew not one person in all of Connecticut. I could disappear and make no excuses to anyone.

So in the spring of 1974, I trekked to a private Walden, to live simply, apart from people, and free. The proximate mission was to examine the ecology of the Connecticut River system, to discover the factors that influenced the distribution of birds along its estuary, but the ultimate mission was otherwise. It was a journey that until now I have not shared, nor have I had any desire to share it, with anyone.

Like the surface of Venus through a small telescope, the marsh appears alien and unknowable. As with Venus's clouds, there is no detectable surface. There are no paths, as water is no more conducive to leading a way than are clouds. They are watery deserts inhabited by the non-human: beings for whom our perspectives are irrelevant. From the moment of entry one is lost, as there is nothing familiar, nothing definite. There is the feeling upon entering of being ferried across the Styx into an underworld.

There are mist-shrouded mornings, sulfur vapors; there are sounds that waft through their atmosphere that would unsettle a departed soul. I can think of no human analogy to explain adequately their nature of existence. As with God's pronouncement to Moses, "I am, who am," so the marsh simply is.

Morning on the marsh is an approximation. There is no morning in the sense that those of us with conscious

Cromwell Meadows

existence view it. Dark and light matter little. The inhabitants begin their day before light, if we can assume that they end their day also, which we cannot. During my explorations, I chose as well to begin before light. I indeed found that my mornings became progressively earlier like other inhabitants of this realm. I realized I understood Herman Melville's character, Bartleby the Scrivener, who increasingly remained at his post until he never left it.

Before I would submit each day to my duties as scientist, I sat in the dark, staring into it and being enshrouded by it. I came to require the dark, the wet and the cold of this time and this place, and found also I increasingly resented having to leave it. It wasn't that the marsh was pleasant, as it was not. As time passed I accumulated infections, welts, stings, bruises. My equipment failed; boots tore, binoculars disappeared, clothes disintegrated, everything human failed. But I had begun to see, or more precisely hear, a glimmer of something else.

Once per week I had to re-enter humanity to obtain groceries. With surprising speed this became immensely unpalatable. I did it as quickly as possible, as it had the effect of an incandescent lamp switched into slumbering darkness. I avoided conversation and returned with haste back to non-human refuge. The shimmer of the single truth disappeared in that world, as does a pond reflection in a wind gust. Only with return to a simplified state could I again catch its glimpse.

I never spoke. I instead listened. There are voices other than ours; their owners did not direct them toward me, but I could eavesdrop, and with practice I could understand an occasional note. My perspective as human progressively receded to its natural place: that of a single voice among many, and those many produced a chorus, a song of being.

We have forgotten this song. It was something I had suspected before, but now that I stood awash in it I was sure. We overwhelm it. Our solitary, blaring cacophony of the mundane drowns it from our ears. We have heard so little of it for so long we have virtually lost our ability to participate. It is not that our remote ancestors ever knew all of it; it is that they knew their part.

This song is one of beginning, of time, of space, the present, the past, death and renewal. Each part is an interval on a graph, a dot on a globe. In 1974 I discovered its existence. Since then I have struggled to decipher its language. I have returned to those marshes now many times, winter and summer, and I continue to do so, always alone, and always in darkness. People presumed I was continuing research on birds. They had not the faintest idea.

I now understand some phrases, but for these I have no human language. Music, like its cousin mathematics, is a different language than that of words. Like those who have tried before me, I expect I will not live long enough to decipher more than a tiny fraction of its composition. You, the readers, might help. If enough of us seek its music, perhaps we can at least learn again our part.

FIELD TRIP
Cromwell Meadows Wildlife Mgmt. Area, Cromwell

Directions: Cromwell Meadows may be reached by traveling north on Rt. 9 to Rt. 99. The first left turn off Rt. 99 is South St. Travel about one mile until a sign indicates a left turn into Cromwell Meadows. Go underneath Rt. 9 to the parking area. Two approaches to visiting may be taken. One is to walk the dirt road out between two portions of the marsh, Round and Boggy Meadow. Another is to go right after the Route 9 underpass and follow the dirt road to the Mattabesset River. A canoe can be launched at this point.

Equipment: At least rubber boots are necessary to explore this wetland and its vicinity. To view it well, hip boots are a better choice. As an alternative, a canoe is an outstanding way to view this extensive area. Mosquitoes and ticks are abundant at certain times of year, so long pants, socks, long sleeve shirts, hats and insect repellent are wise choices. Binoculars and field guides are also helpful for appreciating the area. During the hunting season, the area should be avoided during peak hunting hours (early morning and late afternoon). I recommend that orange reflective clothing be worn during this season.

The habitat: Although Cromwell Meadows is a freshwater marsh, choosing it is a bit like cheating, as it is also tidal throughout much of its extent. However, it is one of the most extensive of Connecticut's freshwater marshes, and over large portions is probably one of the least changed landscapes in the state. Much of its surroundings have been drastically altered, but the marsh persists.

Marshes like these are associated with notable ecological functions, one of the most important of which is their productivity. Freshwater marshes have been reported as being among the most productive of temperate environments, approaching or surpassing even tropical rainforests. This productivity, a measure of the rate at which living material is manufactured, is in large part a consequence of the abundant water and nutrients present in these systems. In tidal habitats in particular, the periodic influx of nutrients and sediments, as well as flushing of wastes, has been associated with high production.

Some of the finest and most extensive examples of riverine marshes in Connecticut may be found at Cromwell Meadows. The meadows are a complex mosaic of plant communities, the distribution of which is to a certain extent related to prevailing water depth. However, as with most things in nature, one single factor cannot explain all that is present.

Predominating over much of the marsh surface are vast stands of River Bulrush (*Scirpus fluviatilis*), which grow in association with the broad-leaved, fleshy Tuckahoe (*Peltandra virginica*). This community evolves as the growing season progresses. In early spring these species appear like little more than green sprouts emerging from tidal mud, but as the growing season progresses the bulrush becomes a "canopy" of sorts, shading the Tuckahoe below it. By late summer the bulrush assumes considerable stature, and may stand six to seven feet tall.

Another striking community that extends over wide areas of Cromwell Meadows is one dominated by Water Horsetail (*Equisetum fluviatile*). Its pale gray-green stands out against the deeper green of River Bulrush. It is a primitive plant, left over from early Earth history when the remote ancestors of today's amphibians ruled the planet. Water Horsetail produces cones (more correctly called strobili) in May that contain spores. The thousands of these strobili-bearing plants drooping beneath heavy dew at dawn is a memorable sight. But as with much that one sees in the marsh, it is an ephemeral vision. By July it has been obliterated by the less common but more robust stems of River Bulrush that overtop it.

Still another community is that characterized by an abundance of the soft-leaved Calamus (*Acorus calamus*). Its lime yellow-green distinguishes it from surrounding marsh vegetation. Superficially appearing like an iris, this relative of Jack-in-the-Pulpit is distinctive among marsh plants in that it releases a sweet scent when its leaves are crushed. Calamus co-occurs with River Bulrush, Tuckahoe and other species, although particularly in earlier spring it can dominate them.

In deeper water, two additional communities may be found. One occurs in sloughs and other deeper spots, and is predominated by Tuckahoe in the virtual absence of River Bulrush. Joining it in these areas are species like Smartweed (*Polygonum* spp.) and Water-dock (*Rumex verticillatus*). The second community is present along the major river (known in the 19th century as the Little River, but presently the Mattabesset River) that flows through the area. At high tide, the river margins are vegetated with plants that, although rooted in soil, have leaves that float on the water's surface. Principal among these are the Bullhead Lily (*Nuphar variegatum*) and Pickerelweed (*Pontederia cordata*). Wild Rice (*Zizania aquatica*), which grows to 10 ft, assumes dominance over much of this area in late summer.

Toward the edge of the marsh and intergrading into the surrounding floodplain forest are bordering areas of Sensitive Fern (*Onoclea sensibilis)*. This species may be found throughout the marsh, but it can form nearly pure stands in less waterlogged areas. Although not as widespread at Cromwell Meadows as at some

Pickerelweed

area marshes, Reed Canary Grass (*Phalaris arundinacea*) also may come to predominate in drier portions of the marsh.

Comparatively uncommon plant associations of Cromwell Meadows include ones that are widespread elsewhere. Stands of Narrow-leaved Cattail (*Typha angustifolia*) have limited distribution, as do stands of Reed (*Phragmites communis*).

An alien species that has invaded the marsh is Purple Loosestrife (*Lythrum salicaria*), a plant of concern to conservationists because it can crowd out natives. However, at Cromwell Meadows it is largely inconspicuous through mid-summer, because it is overtopped by native species until then, although last year's persistent, woody remains are in evidence even in spring. The stable structure of these remains makes them popular nesting platforms for such birds as the Common Yellowthroat, Swamp Sparrow, Red-winged Blackbird and Marsh Wren.

One additional and rather widespread wetland community of Cromwell Meadows is the shrub swamp. It is particularly extensive at that portion of the meadows known as Round Meadow, which from the main parking area is the marsh to the left of the entrance road. I have heard that the construction of Interstate 91 altered water flow in Round Meadow to the point that shrubs invaded the marsh, but I am uncertain of the extent of this change. Dominant species in shrub swamps include stunted specimens of Red Maple (*Acer rubrum*), Buttonball Bush (*Cephalanthus occidentalis*), Speckled Alder (*Alnus rugosa*) and Silky Willow (*Salix sericea*).

Wildlife: As at other Connecticut Valley marshes, the usual contingent of pond frogs (Green Frog, Bullfrog, Pickerel Frog) is joined by the Northern Leopard Frog. The commonest turtle of the meadows is the Eastern Painted Turtle, although the Snapping Turtle also is common. Other turtle species likely to be encountered in the marshes are the Spotted and Musk Turtles. In the adjacent floodplain forest, the Wood Turtle is a characteristic inhabitant. Typical marsh snakes are the Northern Water and Eastern Ribbon Snakes.

The community of freshwater marsh birds is comparatively low in diversity compared with that of upland forest. However, the species occurring in marshes are largely restricted to that habitat. Perhaps the most characteristic of all inhabitants are the rails, a peculiar family of birds with species that rarely fly, are rarely seen, and about which comparatively little is known. The most common rail in Cromwell Meadows is the Virginia Rail, which in some years attains high breeding densities. In other years, such as those with late spring or summer floods, the species may be largely absent. Another species, the Sora, is present as a breeder in the tidal waters of Cromwell Meadows only rarely. It is more consistently and commonly present in nearby non-tidal marshes that are, however, similar to Cromwell Meadows in terms of vegetation.

There is also a rail species that may occur in this area that is otherwise virtually unknown from Connecticut. Once in 1987 on a dreary, gray evening that was turning to rain, I had my first encounter with it. As darkness descended and weather deteriorated, I was at the remotest point in the marsh, so I began the journey back through knee-deep water, struggling across creeks and slippery mud, and stopping periodically to listen. Rain has a way of making marsh voices still, so I was skeptical I would find anything. But amidst my trudging I thought I heard a voice. I splashed to the location where the sounds appeared to come from, and voices continued through the light rain: "kik-kee-do ... kik-kee-do ... kik-kee-do," over and over, with individuals

Virginia Rail

answering each other. There were several in all, just feet from where I was standing. They were the voices of Black Rails.

Even where the Black Rail is common in the Middle Atlantic States, it is a poorly known species. It is tiny and mouse-like, it virtually never flies, and it calls primarily in darkness. Studies of it are few. However, the first description of its nest was made in 19th century Connecticut, its historic northern range limit. In Connecticut, it has been recorded only a handful of times. The birds I found appeared to remain for the summer, but in subsequent years I have not found them again, even during my extensive predawn surveys in 1999 and 2000.

During my extended studies on Connecticut River marshes, one of the observations that quickly became clear was that rarities like the Black Rail tended to differentially collect at Cromwell

Meadows. In fact, when I plotted numbers of rare species present versus marsh size, the largest sites had the highest proportion of rarities. Even after sampling effects were taken into account, the relationship remained. Marsh size itself was a key factor influencing not only the occurrence of rarities, but also the diversity of the entire marsh bird community. When I factored in other habitat attributes like vegetation diversity, marsh size remained the key variable responsible for explaining community diversity. My more recent investigations have verified this relationship, first uncovered during the 1970s and 1980s.

Still another species that is a regular inhabitant of Cromwell Meadows, although it is absent from most of Connecticut is the Least Bittern. Its voice is another one that may be heard in the predawn darkness, although it also may be heard into mid-morning. Its rapid cooing notes are rather like those of the Black-billed Cuckoo, which lives in the adjacent floodplain forest. With practice the voices can be told apart, although not easily. Least Bitterns are most often seen frequenting the edges of creeks.

More widespread but characteristic breeding birds of the freshwater marsh are the Swamp Sparrow, Marsh Wren, Red-winged Blackbird and Mallard. Typical marsh visitors are the Great Blue Heron, Green Heron, Rough-winged Swallow and Tree Swallow. Abundant species of marsh edge thickets are the Yellow Warbler and Common Yellowthroat.

The mammals of freshwater marshes include those species adapted to aquatic environments. The Muskrat is a particularly common and conspicuous inhabitant. The Beaver also is in these areas, particularly along the larger creeks, and Minks are present as well. The characteristic scats of Minks may be found on rocks and logs bordering the marsh, and may be identified by the numerous fish scales that fill them. In the grassy edges of the marshes, Meadow Jumping Mice and Meadow Voles are present.

Closing thoughts: Many of Connecticut's freshwater marshes can trace their beginnings to human activity. The efforts of colonial era farmers in altering watercourses for agricultural purposes remain with us in today's naturally appearing, but actually human-associated habitats. Beaver activity also is responsible for creating marshes.

Some other outstanding examples of largely natural freshwater marsh may be found along the Connecticut River in Chester, Deep River, Lyme (Whalebone Creek, which may be observed easily from an adjacent road), South Windsor and Wethersfield (Wethersfield Meadows).

Swamps 15

W et places have held a special appeal to me ever since I began investigating natural systems. They offer logistical challenges that terrestrial systems do not, so in many instances they are not well known. With their biting insects, leeches, wet, mud and cold, they are traversed by few people. By being able to escape from places where people inhabit, one also escapes some of the environmental disturbance that goes along with human activity. So, at least in some important ways, they are "purer" natural systems to study. Their animal species are often among the most poorly known, so they offer opportunities for discovering new phenomena not previously detected in other environments.

I chose swamps as the environments I would study for my doctoral work, and went on to spend seven years working in the same swamp trying to uncover something of the processes operating in this system. I focused on two obscure and poorly studied species, the Louisiana and Northern waterthrushes, about which little had been written for 20 years. The species presented a compelling problem that could provide new insights into a central tenet of ecological theory. This idea, called the competitive exclusion principle, states that if two species have precisely the same lifestyle they cannot co-exist.

The principle has its basis in the mathematics of population interactions. Ultimately, it is an issue of constructing and interpreting graphs. Every middle school student learns how to plot a straight-line graph and calculate its slope (direction, you might say), but when the graph is that of a curve, finding its slope becomes a problem in calculus. Using the calculus concept of the derivative, it is possible to write an equation that describes the slope of a curve at any point on it. Graphs of population growth tend to be those of curves, so the derivative becomes a powerful tool in understanding the nature of population growth at any point in time. When two populations interact, thereby affecting each other's population growth, calculus concepts also allow us to predict what the outcome of the interaction will be. What they show is that when two species with the same needs compete for limited resources, one species declines to extinction.

Despite this prediction, here in Connecticut we had two bird species, the waterthrushes, which were so similar in appearance that only expert birdwatchers could even tell them apart. Moreover, my preliminary observations had shown that both species inhabited the same swamp, even though they were apparently making a living in much the same way. So, my initial question was, were they really as similar as they seemed? If they were, how did they manage to coexist?

The first step in my investigation was to discover the degree to which these species were similar. I mapped territories, measured the structure of vegetation in these territories, examined how each species fed, measured what foods were available, and also looked at the chemistry of the water in which they fed. I discovered that no matter what parameter I examined, the species had much the same ecology. They, in fact, had completely overlapping territories and often fed in close proximity, yet they virtually ignored each other.

The equations relating to interacting populations have terms, called competition coefficients, which measure the amount that species affect each other. Although it is quite difficult to determine the actual value of these coefficients, their value can be inferred from the amount by which two species ecologically overlap. I found that the two waterthrushes overlapped 80-100 percent in all measures I made, implying that their competition coefficients were very high. I therefore concluded that the species really were as similar as they seemed, and yet coexisted without any apparent negative interaction. In other words, I could find no evidence that competition occurred between them despite their

Louisiana Waterthrush

similarity.

This set the stage for the next phase of the investigation. The so-called competition equations are relevant only if there is something to compete over. What my findings were implying was that nothing might be in short supply, so the species could be very similar and still not negatively interact.

Food (various kinds of invertebrates) appeared to be the most likely resource to be in limited supply. It certainly wasn't living space, as I had shown the waterthrushes could live together. I had already demonstrated that both species fed almost exclusively from water during the first half of the breeding season, so the water appeared to be the best place to search for evidence of competition. To maximize my probability of detecting competition, I picked an exceptionally dry spring with low water levels (thus limited feeding areas) to minimize the amount of food available. I then excluded waterthrushes from feeding in parts of the swamp, and compared the food supply there with areas where they actively fed. I found no clear differences between these areas. Hence, the birds appeared to be having little effect on food even when it was most likely to be limiting.

I further looked at the details of exactly what the two species ate. By putting wild birds into a semi-captive situation (I built a giant portable bird cage right in the swamp), I was able to examine them at close range. From this, I determined that some subtle differences existed in the type and size of foods the species ate, although these aspects of their diets still overlapped by 60 percent. This reduced level of overlap compared with my previous studies could suggest that diets diverged because of competition, but in light of my findings for food availability and the continued absence of any aggression between the species (a clear indicator of competition), an alternate explanation was more plausible. The differences in food choice showed a close relationship to species differences in size, so limited divergence in food use could be explained simply as a consequence of small differences in body size. In short, even after years of searching, there was no compelling evidence for the existence of competition between these species. In this instance it did not appear that conditions producing competition existed, and the species could, therefore, exhibit great ecological similarity.

So, there is indeed much to be learned about ecological processes by examining the details of what transpires in swamps. Before I proceed to describing a field trip to a swamp, however, there are several additional aspects of them that deserve mention. Swamps typically develop in topographic depressions that are poorly drained. They are usually associated with streams, so have some water flowing through them. In such areas, muck soils develop that are waterlogged for extended periods. Unlike the peat substrate of bogs, these muck soils have a large mineral component. Swamps also may develop in areas where the water table intersects the surface, or in places underlain by an impervious layer like clay, which does not allow drainage of water.

Although poorly drained, swamps in Connecticut are not characterized by deep water, and indeed local trees and shrubs can grow only in shallower situations. Pools of standing water from several inches to about one foot in depth are typical, particularly in spring, although by late summer many pools dry out. Higher spots called hummocks occur throughout the swamp, and it is on these that many woody plants grow. Hummocks may be derived from the decaying logs of fallen trees, the remains of upturned roots and their associated soil, or protruding rocks.

FIELD TRIP
Nehantic State Forest, East Lyme

Directions: Travel north on Rt. 85 in Montville to Grassy Hill Rd. Go left at the junction, and drive about 2.4 miles until a parking area for Nehantic State Forest appears on the right. A dirt road leads into the forest, and this road can be used to explore swamps in the area.

Equipment: Much of this area can be explored from the road. However, the more adventurous may wish to have rubber boots to explore the wetlands further. Mosquitoes, black flies and ticks are abundant at certain times of year, so long pants, socks, long sleeve shirts, hats and insect repellent are wise choices. Binoculars and field guides are also helpful for appreciating the area. During the hunting season, the area should be avoided during peak hunting hours (early morning and late afternoon). I recommend that orange reflective clothing be worn during this season.

The habitat: The rough topography in this section of Nehantic State Forest yields upland forests interspersed with areas of stream and swamp. Due to the area's landforms and juxtaposition of wet areas, it is particularly attractive woodland.

Swampy spots are present directly adjacent to the parking area, although a more interesting location may be reached by walking about a mile down the dirt road to where a swampy stream crosses. The trees Red Maple (*Acer rubrum*) and Yellow Birch (*Betula lutea*) are present commonly. Other deciduous trees characteristic of moist swamp borders are also present, like White Ash (*Fraxinus americana*) and Shagbark Hickory (*Carya ovata*). Less common swamp trees like Black Ash (*F. nigra*) and Shadbush (*Amelanchier canadensis*) are present as well.

Conifers occurring in swamps include the Eastern Hemlock (*Tsuga canadensis*) and Eastern White Pine (*Pinus strobus*). These tend to be more common in northern areas, but they may be found in Nehantic State Forest. In contrast, the Atlantic White-cedar (*Chamaecyparis thyoides*) is present in northern and southern Connecticut, although it is most typical of the eastern third of the state. At Nehantic State Forest, specimens of Atlantic White-cedar show the elegant cylindrical crowns and tight, winding stripes of bark characteristic of mature trees.

Marsh Marigold

Still another species associated with wetter areas is the Yellow Poplar (*Liriodendron tulipifera*). Although it does not grow in swamps, it is characteristic of their borders. It is one of the region's largest and fastest growing trees, and one of our few trees to produce showy flowers. The green and orange blooms cover branches in late spring, and the generalized flowers of separate sepals and petals hint that the species is one of great antiquity. Indeed, members of its family, the Magnolias, are among the more primitive of flowering plants, and specimens of trees virtually identical to the modern Yellow Poplar exist as fossils from much earlier times.

The understory of swamps is characteristically dense, in part because shallow-rooted swamp trees tend to fall over and leave gaps in the swamp canopy. The tendency of trees to fall also helps to make swamps the tangled morass they are famous for being. Species like Winterberry (*Ilex verticillata*), Highbush Blueberry (*Vaccinium corymbosum*), Witherod (*Viburnum cassinoides*), Arrowwood (*V. recognitum*), Spicebush (*Lindera benzoin*), Mountain Holly (*Nemopanthus mucronata*), Speckled Alder (*Alnus rugosa*), Sweet Pepperbush (*Clethra alnifolia*), Swamp Azalea (*Rhododendron viscosum*), Pink Azalea (*R. nudiflorum*) and Mountain Laurel (*Kalmia latifolia*) all are present in swamp environments.

The herbaceous flora of the swamp is also a rich one. Among

flowering herbs, Marsh Marigold (*Caltha palustris*) is one that blooms in early spring. Its leaves are edible, and some people prepare them like spinach. Other common swamp herbs include the Golden Ragwort (*Senecio aureus*), Swamp Saxifrage (*Saxifraga pensylvanica*), Marsh Blue Violet (*Viola cucullata*), Water Parsnip (*Sium suave*), and Jewelweed (*Impatiens capensis*). *Sphagnum* mosses form a cover over many hummocks and less submerged spots.

An abundant herb of the swamp is the Skunk Cabbage (*Symplocarpus foetidus*), which is a relative of Jack-in-the-pulpit (*Arisaema triphyllum*). In early spring, Skunk Cabbage produces a reddish, hooded cluster of flowers that precedes the leaves. When the leaves later unfold, they are among the largest in the forest, and when broken they emit a skunk-like odor. A showy, white-hooded relative of Skunk Cabbage that flowers later in spring is the Wild Calla (*Calla palustris*). Another species similar in appearance to Skunk Cabbage, although unrelated to it, is the False Hellebore (*Veratrum viride*), which in addition to having large leaves produces a large cluster of green flowers.

Ferns are an abundant component of the herbaceous flora, and include Cinnamon (*Osmunda cinnamomea*), Royal (*O. regalis*), Sensitive (*Onoclea sensibilis*) and Crested Ferns (*Dryopteris cristata*). "Fern allies," the horsetails, also occur in swamps. Like ferns, horsetails are so primitive that not only do they not produce flowers, they don't even produce seeds like conifers. Their most conspicuous means of reproduction is by means of spores, much like the mosses. During the Age of Amphibians, Carboniferous times, horsetails formed important elements of the forest canopy. Most modern species are rarely more that two feet tall.

A species of horsetail that occurs in swamps is the Wood Horsetail (*Equisetum sylvaticum*). It is a lacy species with whorls of spindly branches that make it appear like a fairytale plant. Another horsetail more typical of swamp openings and areas along rivers is the Scouring Rush (*E. hiemale*). Instead of being delicate, it has a thick, coarse stem, no branches, and it is usually crowned by a spore-bearing structure that looks somewhat like a cone. Because of its coarseness, people once used it to clean pots.

Wildlife: The tiny aquatic organisms that live in swamps include some of the more delicate and interesting creatures of the invertebrate world. Among the more primitive of the legged animals (arthropods) are the aquatic sowbugs (*Asellus* sp.), which are actually not bugs at all but in a group called the isopods. Their segmented bodies resemble their remote and extinct relatives, the trilobites, which were common inhabitants of early seas. The abundant aquatic snail of the swamp, *Physa,* is a representative of another invertebrate group of great antiquity. It and *Asellus* may be found easily by turning over dead leaves in swamp pools.

The insect life of the swamp includes some of the most appealing as well as some of the most noxious of invertebrates. They are rather sophisticated creatures compared to the sowbugs, although they themselves can be divided into more primitive and more advanced groups. Many of the more primitive insects have a life cycle in which the juveniles, or nymphs, appear at least somewhat like the adults they will become. The nymphs are aquatic, and the adults are typically flying, often short-lived forms. More advanced forms may undergo a complete metamorphosis from a wormy-looking aquatic larval stage to an air-breathing adult stage.

Among the primitive insects are the Mayflies (*Ephemeroptera*), so named because many kinds reach the flying, adult stage during May. The adults are delicate, short-lived creatures whose primary mission is to lay eggs in the water from which they recently emerged. The aquatic nymphs are strangely beautiful creatures under the lens of a dissecting microscope. This water-breathing stage is characterized by rows of feathery gills lining the abdomen. Many species are characteristic of fast-flowing water, but others live in the quiet water of swamps.

Other nymphs present in swamp pools are those of the Dragonflies (*Odonata*). The somewhat fixed-winged, primitive adult stages fill the air of the swamp in late summer, but in spring the large and ferociously predatory nymphs can be shocking things to discover among the leaves of swamp pools.

Caddisflies (*Trichoptera*) are a more advanced insect group that has a flying adult stage and a water-breathing aquatic larval stage. The larvae often construct protective cases that surround all of their soft bodies except for their head. Predators like the Waterthrushes have, however, learned to extract the nymphs from these cases.

Other insects showing complete metamorphoses are the beetles (*Coleoptera*) and flies (*Diptera*). Some beetle larvae like Dytiscids are predatory forms. Diptera include the abundant midges and such infamous swamp dwellers as mosquitos and black flies.

Swamps are good habitats for amphibians and, consequently, a number of species use them. Swamp pools offer many of the same advantages as vernal (temporary) ponds for breeding amphibians. They can be too small and unconnected to larger bodies of water to afford access to predators like fish, so they provide some refuge from predators for developing amphibians.

Every early spring, amphibians begin moving to vernal ponds and swamps to lay their eggs. The species that commonly reach the breeding areas first include the Wood Frog, Spring Peeper and Spotted Salamander. Later in spring, the American and Fowler's Toad begin to breed, and the Gray Tree Frog arrives still later. Still other species, like the Blue-spotted and Jefferson's Salamanders breed in more limited areas in the state, and one species, the Marbled Salamander, breeds in fall. Species like the Green, Bull and Pickerel Frog may be found in swamps and larger areas of open water not only in the breeding season but also throughout the summer.

Reptiles are also characteristic inhabitants of swamps. The Northern Water Snake is present, particularly where larger areas of open water are found. The Eastern Painted Turtle and Snapping Turtle are also very common in areas with significant open water. The Spotted Turtle is still another typical swamp inhabitant, and a less known and more secretive species, the Musk Turtle, inhabits muddy-bottomed areas.

The birds of the swamp include several species that are specialists for the swamp environment. The Louisiana Waterthrush usually occurs where there is some moving water, and the swampy streams of Nehantic State Forest provide very suitable habitat for it. Within these habitats, it often chooses as its nest site the upturned roots of fallen trees. Its close relative, the Northern Waterthrush, is generally less common in southern than northern Connecticut, in part because it approaches its southern range limit in our state. It prefers swamps with a high proportion of coniferous cover, although it also occurs in largely deciduous swamps.

Species of openings in the swamp canopy include the Common Yellowthroat, Blue-winged Warbler, Rose-breasted Grosbeak, American Redstart and Gray Catbird. The Veery is a very common inhabitant of the moist forests bordering the swamp, where it nests on the ground, although it often moves into the swamp to feed.

In Nehantic State Forest, several species may be found whose populations are concentrated in southern Connecticut. One

Red-backed Vole

is the Acadian Flycatcher, which occurs in the swamp itself. Another is the Cerulean Warbler, a species that makes use of the moist, mature forests surrounding the swamp. Still another is the Hooded Warbler, which uses the dense thickets present in swamp environments. In contrast to these species, the

Winter Wren is largely restricted to northern Connecticut during the breeding season. However, it may be found in swamp thickets in the southern portion of the state during the winter months.

Certain mammals show particularly close associations with the swamp environment. Both the Mink and River Otter may be found there. The presence of Minks is often revealed by the scats they leave on fallen logs and rocks, which are often easily identified because they are composed largely of fish scales. Another abundant small mammal is the Red-backed Vole. Water Shrews also inhabit swamps, although I have had little success finding them there. Other species, like the Gray Squirrel, Red Squirrel and Chipmunk may inhabit swamps, but they are not restricted to them.

Closing thoughts: A number of fine examples of Atlantic White-cedar swamps are found around eastern Connecticut. One excellent spot open to the public (although it appears to be a bog rather than a swamp) in which Atlantic White-cedar mixes with Black Spruce (*Picea mariana*) may be found opposite the Windham Airport on Rt. 6 in Windham. The area is so tangled that it is extremely difficult to traverse, but it may be explored easily from an old railroad bed (now a hiking trail) that lies behind it.

Another spectacular swamp exhibiting mature Atlantic White-cedar growing with an understory of Mountain Laurel and Rhododendron (*Rhododendron maximum*) is found in Pachaug State Forest, Voluntown. This area is called the Rhododendron Sanctuary, and is easily explored by walking the boardwalk that has been built through it. Rhododendron is an abundant tree of the Appalachian Mts., but its distribution in the Northeast is spotty. It occurs only locally in southern New England, and it has a separate population in Nova Scotia. This distribution is likely to be at least in part an artifact of events that unfolded at the close of glacial times. In our area, I have found individuals scattered throughout the state, but much of the local population appears to be in southeastern Connecticut and southern Rhode Island. It grows as a small tree in the Appalachians, but in the Rhododendron Sanctuary and other area swamps it is a large, sprawling shrub. When it flowers in early July, it provides one of the showiest displays of blooms that may be seen in any natural area in the state.

Other favorite swamps where I go exploring for unusual species are in northern Connecticut. The swampy stream that borders the paved road through Bigelow Hollow State Park in Union is typical of many hemlock-white pine swamps in the region, and may be easily observed from the road. The dense understory of this swamp is home to such typically northern-associated species as the Canada Warbler, Northern Waterthrush, and Winter Wren. Another remote swamp, Keep Swamp, which is at the summit of Canaan Mountain in Canaan, can be reached only by a long hike. It is more open in character, and the vicinity is home to still another northern species, the Yellow-bellied Sapsucker.

Bogs 16

After spending a day visiting several bogs in preparation for writing this chapter, I awoke that night out of a dream about death. It was a dream I have had many times. I shook off its perennially dark horror by contemplating its subject: my own mortality, what I have done with the fleeting time available to me, and what I will accomplish before there is no time. I thought about Franz Kafka's literary character Joseph K, who awoke on the morning of his thirtieth birthday to find himself arrested-Kafka's metaphor of life's judgment.

I last explored these bogs in Northwest Connecticut a lifetime ago, when time did not yet seem so finite. I had examined all my field notes from those earlier expeditions in preparation for the trip, all written in my own hand, all looking as if I had just taken them, although they were now incongruously old. Looking at them made me think of my father. When he was very old and with little

169

remaining vision, he sat with me one night talking about George Patton, whom he knew. He described the buttons on Patton's uniform, his helmet, his pearl-handled revolvers, all as if he were clearly looking at him that instant. He concluded by saying that it all didn't seem that long ago. The nearly 60 intervening years were irrelevant. Indeed. I realized also that I could still see where I was standing as I wrote my notes, see the pencil in my hands, feel the exhilaration of being in my first real bog.

Time is a troublesome quantity. Newton thought it was independent and universal, but Einstein demonstrated that it was connected to space, much as height is connected to length and width, and that the nature of time was relative to how one viewed it. The French writer Jean Paul Sartre wrote further that time consisted of wide, soft instants, and in doing so hinted that time exists as particles. The past is a chemical illusion of the brain, and we exist only in the instant that is the present. Small wonder, then, that we struggle with time and our experience of it. We have memories, but where they exist in time is unclear. We first experience events in a present instant, and they forevermore appear to exist in that present. However, what we do in reality is move linearly through time, from the moment of our inception until death overtakes us, and in this we, and bogs, have a connection.

Bogs are dying places. As with us, from their own life comes death. They are places that elicit dreams of death, and cause one to contemplate the journey from the beginning to its end. Is there a point to it, a goal, or is it without meaning? Bogs are, in fact, awash in death; they are often monumentally old places, filled with decay, and yet they strangely appear to change little over time. Just as a small interval on the graph of a curve appears as a straight line, so the interval of a bog we see over our lives appears constant. The bogs I visited were precisely as I remembered them 30 years earlier. We simply don't live at the same scale that do bogs. Yet, like us, they are born, they age, and they ultimately die.

Cranberry

Old bogs are the remains of other times: times of ice, of Caribou, and of Wooly Mammoths. It was along the edges of meltwater pools in a landscape emerging from frozen stillness that the first plant life colonized them. Some of those plants, notably the sedges, extended in mats over the surface of the pond. In doing so, they gave birth to a new type of environment.

To a certain extent, bogs work opposite to the way that most habitats do. Instead of the physical environment setting the parameters of the emerging biological landscape, in bogs the living components are conspicuously involved in creating their own environment. They do this through death. Once a vegetation mat is established, decaying plant material annually accumulates on it, and plant debris rain into the pond below. The stagnant pond accumulates these debris in an environment virtually devoid of oxygen, making its depths a mausoleum. The materials build into a thick layer that in the absence of oxygen turns into a semi-preserved substance called peat.

On the surface of the bog, which is notoriously low in essential plant nutrients, a procession of colonization events occur by increasingly more complex plant forms. In the beginning, it is plants like the sedges and thick, spongy mats of the moss *Sphagnum*. A host of other herbaceous plants colonize as well, with grasses like Cotton Grass being particularly conspicuous. As bogs age, their vegetation mat thickens, producing a substrate more suitable for colonization by woody plants. Notably, some of the same straggling woody species that colonize bogs, like Creeping Snowberry, are the same species that survive in the far north and at high elevations in mountains. In short, they are species adapted to environmental extremes.

The herbaceous and shrubby components of the bog flora extend out across the pond at middle age, and toward the edge trees become established. As with the bog itself, the identity of these trees hearkens back to an earlier epoch when Connecticut's emerging landscape was vegetated for the first time. The blue-black spires of Black Spruce contrast with the open, lime green crowns of Tamarack in this meeting ground of upland and wetland. Such trees are still today more characteristic of the far north, and are found with us principally in bogs. In old age, the pond fills completely with peat, and the curious quaking surface of the young bog (like the surface of a trampoline because it actually floats over the pond) is replaced with a more stable surface. Trees may extend to the center of old bogs, although herbaceous and shrubby areas may also remain extensive.

Old bogs will be the focus of this field trip. They are the ones with the most direct connection with the emergence of life in post glacial-Connecticut and, thus, in many ways they are the most interesting. There are younger bogs in our region, and indeed bog formation proceeds today anew in places like beaver ponds.

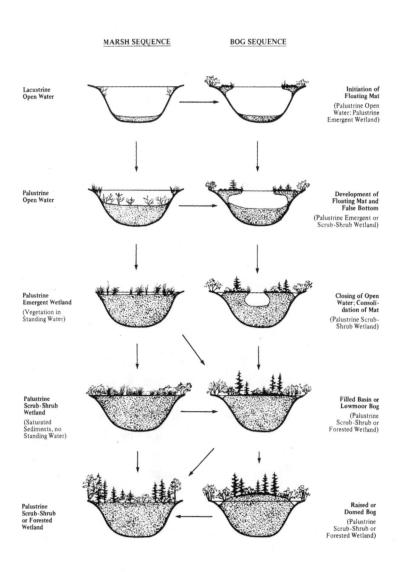

MARSH SEQUENCE   BOG SEQUENCE

Lacustrine Open Water

Initiation of Floating Mat
(Palustrine Open Water; Palustrine Emergent Wetland)

Palustrine Open Water

Development of Floating Mat and False Bottom
(Palustrine Emergent or Scrub-Shrub Wetland)

Palustrine Emergent Wetland
(Vegetation in Standing Water)

Closing of Open Water; Consolidation of Mat
(Palustrine Scrub-Shrub Wetland)

Palustrine Scrub-Shrub Wetland
(Saturated Sediments, no Standing Water)

Filled Basin or Lowmoor Bog
(Palustrine Scrub-Shrub or Forested Wetland)

Palustrine Scrub-Shrub or Forested Wetland

Raised or Domed Bog
(Palustrine Scrub-Shrub or Forested Wetland)

Courtesy, Connecticut Department of Environmental Protection, copyright 1991.

FIELD TRIP
Black Spruce Bog, Mohawk State Forest, Goshen

Directions: From Rt. 4 west, go through Goshen center until a State Forest sign indicates a left turn into Mohawk State Forest. If you reach the junction of Routes 4 and 43, you have gone too far. Follow the unpaved road until signs appear for Black Spruce Bog. Make a left turn onto Mohawk Mt. Road (also unpaved), and on the right there is a parking area next to State Forest buildings. Cross the road to where a short path leads to a boardwalk through the two acre site. People bring baby strollers onto the boardwalk, so consider the area extremely accessible.

Equipment: Long pants, a hat, socks, sneakers and insect repellent are recommended in warmer months. Binoculars and field guides are useful at any season.

The habitat: Black Spruce Bog contains mature trees throughout most of it, including species not restricted to bogs. The bog canopy consists of the conifers Black Spruce (*Picea mariana*) and Tamarack (*Larix laricina*). Moreover, Eastern White Pine (*Pinus strobus*) and Eastern Hemlock (*Tsuga canadensis*) are present. The ubiquitous Red Maple (*Acer rubrum*) joins with these conifers as a common associate, as does Yellow Birch (*Betula lutea*). Mature trees 50 to 60 ft tall are present throughout much of the site.

The bog has a well-developed and densely shrubby understory, which is typical of wooded wetlands in general. Characteristic tall shrubs include Winterberry (*Ilex verticillata*), Highbush Blueberry (*Vaccinium corymbosum*) and Black Chokeberry (*Aronia melanocarpa*). Low shrubs and trailing woody plants include Leatherleaf (*Chamadaphne calyculata*), Small Cranberry (*Vaccinium oxycoccos*), Creeping Snowberry (*Gaultheria hispidula*) and Sheep Laurel (*Kalmia angustifolia*). Strangely enough, this last species is also at home in very dry, sandy, acidic soils. Other shrubs to look for in this and other bogs are the various species of Viburnum (including *Viburnum cassinoides, V. lentago, V. recognitum* and *V.*

opulus), Spicebush (*Lindera benzoin*), Speckled Alder (*Alnus rugosa*), Mountain Laurel (*Kalmia latifolia*) and American Elder (*Sambucus canadensis*), as well as the bog specialties Labrador Tea (*Ledum groenlandicum*) and Bog Rosemary (*Andromeda glaucophylla*).

Signs posted at the entrance to the bog also tout the presence of the shrub Mountain Holly (*Nemopanthus mucronata*) as being quite unusual. As its name suggests, this holly relative is a characteristic shrub of the northern Appalachian Mountains (south as far as West Virginia), although it also grows into the far north. I have found it in moist upland forests in the Appalachians, but with us I find it entirely restricted to wooded wetlands and their borders. It is a nondescript species that easily escapes detection. Its toothed, oval leaves are similar to those of other bog shrubs like Winterberry (a true holly), but during summer its leaf bases (petioles) are distinctly plum colored. Although it is an interesting species, it is actually not particularly unusual. It is present in many swamps and bogs even in southern Connecticut.

The herbaceous component of the bog is punctuated by species characteristic of bog environments. *Sphagnum* moss is ubiquitous, and the carnivorous plants Round-leaved Sundew (*Drosera rotundifolia*) and Pitcher Plant (*Sarracenia purpurea*) appear fairly commonly. One strategy for living in the nutrient poor environment of the bog is to derive nutrients from elsewhere, and this is just what these plants do. The sundews have glistening drops of sticky gel on projecting leaf hairs. Insects are attracted to the gel, and once they are entangled in it, the plant digests them and derives nutrients from their tissues. Pitcher plants actually are pitcher-shaped, and are filled with a sweet fluid that also attracts insects. Once an insect lands on the downward-projecting hairs of the inside of the pitcher, it makes its way to the fluid, where it is digested.

Another notable herbaceous plants is Cotton Grass (*Eriophorum spissum*), named for the cottony seed heads it produces in mid-late summer. Goldthread (*Coptis groenlandica*), named for its gold colored roots, is an abundant species in the bog as well. Also present commonly are Cinnamon (*Osmunda cinnamomea*) and Crested Ferns (*Dryopteris cristata*), Swamp Saxifrage (*Saxifraga pensylvanica*), Clintonia (*Clintonia borealis*), Bunchberry (*Cornus canadensis*) and Sensitive Fern (*Onoclea sensibilis*). Although characteristic of moister environments, some of these species are not restricted to wetlands.

Wildlife: I once extensively sampled the aquatic life of a bog as part of a study I was conducting on prey available to bog-dwelling birds, and found comparatively little present because of the low nutrient, low oxygen, and highly acidic nature of bog water. However, some of the species exhibited specific adaptations to the bog environment. The larvae (juvenile stage) of Midges, tiny aquatic insects that spend much of their life cycle in water, were blood red. The red was from hemoglobin, the same molecule that makes our blood red. This hemoglobin was involved in helping them extract sufficient oxygen from their environment to sustain them. Other notable aquatic creatures were the predatory aquatic larvae of beetles called Dytiscids and an unusual group of beetles called the Helodids. Larvae of a fly relative that go by the rather vulgar name of rat-tailed maggots also were present. The "rat tails" functioned somewhat like snorkels for deriving oxygen from the air. Present as well were the larvae of mosquitoes, which exhibit their own adaptations for low oxygen waters.

Amphibians present in bogs include the usual pond frogs like Green, Bull and Pickerel Frogs. One of the more notable species that inhabits bogs is the Four-toed Salamander, which is reported to live beneath the mats of *Sphagnum* moss. I have never relished the idea of ripping up yards of *Sphagnum* to search for them, so I have not found them in this way, although on rainy nights I have found them walking about at the edges of swamps. It might be expected that reptiles like the Bog Turtle would occur in bogs, but in reality they appear to be absent from Connecticut's acidic bogs and are instead largely restricted to wetlands underlain by calcareous rocks. However, the Spotted Turtle does inhabit bogs. Moreover, I have observed the Wood Turtle, a comparatively terrestrial member of the turtle order, to occur at least at the edge of boggy environments.

Pitcher Plant

Bird life within the confines of the bog includes in summer species like the Northern Waterthrush. Although not restricted to bogs, it is characteristic of mossy, coniferous wetlands. A frequent associate of the Waterthrush is the Canada Warbler, particularly where Mountain Laurel is a common understory shrub. Where bogs become open due to uprooting of trees (shallowly rooted trees commonly fall over in swampy environments), the Nashville Warbler may be present as well. Other species encountered in the bog or at the edges of it include the Veery, Yellow-bellied Sapsucker (open bogs) and Winter Wren. In winter I have found that Saw-whet Owls use bog conifers as roost trees, and I have found apparent breeders in such environments as well.

Perhaps the most abundant mammal I have found in boggy environments is the Red-backed Vole, although at one site I observed the rather uncommon Water Shrew appearing to run across the surface of a shallow pool. As might be expected, the Southern Bog Lemming is described as occurring in such places as well, although I have never successfully captured one myself. On occasion I have observed Minks (once capturing a Chipmunk!) and even a River Otter in boggy areas, but I would not consider bogs to be prime habitats for them.

Closing thoughts: Other types of bog environments also occur in Connecticut. An interesting one that appears to be of bog origin is opposite the Windham Airport on R. 6 in Windham. An abandoned railroad bed borders the bog, and is available for public access. In eastern Connecticut, the southerly-distributed conifer Atlantic White-cedar (*Chamaecyparis thyoides*) can become an important bog and swamp species. It predominates at this site, but some Black Spruce is also present, along with typical bog shrubs like Winterberry, Highbush Blueberry, and Mountain Holly. It is an extremely dense and tangled environment, so plan on remaining on the railroad bed to observe it.

I began with dark thought about bogs. The lifespan of bogs is finite, as is our own. However, in their present they are also glorious, in their shapes, their colors, and their variety. As I explored the bogs for this chapter I found they were new and wonderful all over again; it was as if I had encountered life-long, and long lost, friends.

Beaches 17

Estanislao Taisacan is a chain smoking, beetlenut chewing Pacific Islander with an affection for cold beer and a propensity for hot temper. He and I were a universe apart in culture, yet more alike in substantive ways than different. We were connected by a common passion, and connected as well in ways that few others could understand. Neither Stan nor I ever should have existed; the probability that we both would, and would further come to know each other, fell within the realm of remote probability.

Stan is a native of the tropical island of Rota, a dot in the Marianas archipelago in the western Pacific. It is a volcanic mountaintop rising from a sea bluer than any blue I would have thought possible. His ancestors colonized this island some time long before written records began. They persisted in the face of successive Spanish and German occupations, but by 1944 faced extinction at the hand of the Japanese.

Stan once took me to the spot where it was to occur, through tiers of an orchid-encrusted jungle that previously for me had existed only in fantasy. He brought me to a plateau, riddled with deep shafts cut into its rocks during an era of phosphate mining. His parents, along with every other islander,

The author in the Rota jungle

were to be herded to this spot and cast down the shafts. All available resources on Rota were to be reserved for the occupying Japanese army. Only relentless bombing and strafing by American warplanes prevented them from carrying out their plan. As we walked over the area, I knelt and gathered a handful of American 50 caliber machine gun shells. They were everywhere. I wanted to save some, as they were the instruments that permitted me to know Stan.

Ten thousand miles to the west, also in 1944, my father was running up a beach in Italy. He described it to me once. A military landing began with men climbing down netting hung from the pitching decks of troop ships. Reaching the landing craft below involved jumping from the netting. Most made it, others missed and simply disappeared beneath the waves. Upon reaching the beach, those disembarking first met the remains of Seabees drifting in the surf. Pop said he could not at first understand why everyone running up the beach was tripping. But as he looked back and saw he was one of few still standing, he realized they had not tripped. That was all he said; I did not have the heart to ask about it further.

Some months later, beneath the monastery at Monte Cassino, Italy, a German plane dropped a bomb on the American lines. Pop dove on one side of a Jeep, others dove on the opposite side. Those others were killed. He had been riddled by shrapnel, but a small address book in his chest pocket slowed a fragment's passage just enough to prevent penetration of his heart. The fragment and book remained with him the rest of his life.

So, the probability of the combined existence of Estanislao Taisacan and me was certainly small. Yet we did, and during the early 1990s we turned the fact of our existence and our common sensibilities toward doing one good thing. There was a bird, the Rota White-eye. It was bland, tiny and virtually unknown to science. In Stan's lifetime it had gone from common and widespread to shrinking toward extinction. Hardly anyone was paying attention. I scratched my head over the disinterest; here was a species that had evolved in isolation for a million years. It was a surviving remnant of island prehistory. Once gone, still another piece of the ecological-evolutionary puzzle would be forever lost.

In prehistory, Stan's ancestors had presided over the extinction of greater than half the island's fauna. There were flightless ibises, giant white-eyes, ducks, parrots, parrot-finches; all manner of species today known only from their bones. Stan would instead stem the ongoing tide. Together, we developed an approach toward stopping the extinctions with the white-eye.

Our first step was to learn the basic biology of this unknown species. We mapped distributions and population density by performing population surveys. By following birds, we determined that the Rota White-eye lived in flocks that to a certain extent were extended families. Flocks occupied a distinct home range, and remained within this home range over time. Birds typically used forest canopy, but could occupy habitats from forest openings to alien bamboo stands. In these habitats they fed upon insects, fruit, nectar and seeds.

We next turned our attention toward identifying the agent of the species' decline. An introduced, aggressively predatory bird, the Black Drongo, appeared a likely candidate. When we plotted drongo distributions versus those of white-eyes, it was clear that drongos were common where white-eyes were absent. Where white-eyes were present, drongos were least common. Our observations of drongos within present white-eye range further showed that they relentlessly pursued the tiny white-eyes. The white-eye habit of feeding in the forest canopy and flying above it made birds particularly susceptible to predation. We further noted that during the years when drongo populations were rapidly expanding (the 1950s), white-eye populations were plummeting.

With the likely agent of decline identified, we set to work eliminating it. We found funds for ammunition, and instituted a control program for drongos. We shot them at places they congregated, and we in particular eliminated them from within the remaining range of the white-eye. It was appalling work. Days of nonstop killing weighed upon me. I found myself in the position of shooting adults, and then shooting their young as they hovered above. Within two weeks we made a dramatic dent in drongo numbers, and we freed the few remaining flocks of white-eyes from constant harassment by nearby drongos.

It was a lesson in how real conservation often proceeds. There were the two of us, several aging shotguns, and a rusting truck. We were what stood between the Rota White-eye and forevermore extinction. It was the time when I first realized something I have now stated many times: every endangered species needs a champion. Without individuals to champion the cause of a species in danger, that species may disappear with hardly any notice being paid. Today the Rota White-eye's future is still precarious, but it has not become extinct. Through our efforts, our prodding for the institution of a captive breeding program, and the efforts of those who have followed us, its chances of survival are far brighter than when we began.

So, what is to be gleaned from all this? This chapter is to

concern Connecticut beaches, and not remote islands. Indeed, nearly everything of the Connecticut landscape is so far removed from the world of tropical islands that it is hard to imagine both existing simultaneously. Yet they do share a connection, and the connection is in the phrase forevermore extinction. Before my service in the Pacific, I had not known the reality of holding the fate of an entire race of beings in my own, personal hands. Such knowledge has the effect of altering one's world view; it is, in essence, an epiphany. Much of what I have written in this entire volume has been influenced by that knowledge. Confronting real endangerment is dire business; it is the business of bringing back from the abyss species poised to slip beneath floodwaters. I cannot use the term "endangered" lightly, and I do not do so in this book.

Connecticut is fortunate to have few species facing the stultifying reality of genuine extinction. There are, however, a few, and some make their precarious homes on our region's beaches. In fact, it is not solely the species that occupy this habitat that are in peril, but the entire environment is one that is reeling from the same insults that have brought island communities and species like the Rota White-eye to their knees: overwhelming human presence, exotic introductions, habitat destruction, and the effects of predators on species with few defenses to combat them.

Field Trip
Milford Point Refuge, Milford

Directions: Milford Point may be reached by taking Route 1 in Milford to Naugatuck Ave. If you are coming from the east and reach the Housatonic River, you have gone too far. After about ½ mile turn right onto Milford Point Rd., which leads to the Connecticut Audubon Society's refuge at Milford Point. Adjacent to this refuge and encompassing the tip of Milford Point is McKinney National Wildlife Refuge.

Equipment: This site is easily accessible with no special

equipment. Mosquitoes and ticks are abundant at certain times of the year, so long pants, socks, long sleeve shirts, hats and insect repellent are wise choices. Binoculars and field guides are also helpful. Guides are particularly useful for distinguishing the numerous species of marine invertebrates that may be found in this environment. Although Milford Point is a refuge, the surrounding waters and marshes are open to hunting, so orange reflective clothing should be worn during hunting season.

The habitat: Only a handful of Connecticut beaches still exist in their natural state. Most are overrun with beach houses and other development. The natural communities that occupy them are similarly limited in extent, and are often degraded by human trampling and introduced weeds. Despite this, it is still possible to examine some good examples of natural beach phenomena within the state's boundaries.

Milford Point is a fine but sad remnant of the Connecticut shoreline's former wildness. As are many of the remaining undeveloped areas of coastline, it is cut off from other natural uplands by an ocean of urbanization. Its saving feature is that behind it in the estuarine waters of the Housatonic River are some of the most extensive examples of low salt marsh (*Spartina alterniflora*) found in Connecticut.

Geologically, Milford Point is a sand spit, a sandy extension of upland bordering the shoreline. It is formed from current-deposited sand as coastal headlands upcurrent from it erode. Debris left at the shoreline during glacial times provide many of the easily eroded materials that are transported to form beaches. A notable feature of the sand at this and other Connecticut beaches is the abundant presence of garnet crystals, which gives the sand a red appearance. These garnets have been eroded from local crystalline rocks.

Because of the nature of the processes that give rise to them, beaches are rather ephemeral features. Examination of historic coastal charts invariably shows that such features change shape and even disappear over time. Large coastal storms in particular are agents of profound change.

The classic oceanic beach profile of the northeastern U.S. begins with the berm, that area of beach above high tide that is largely devoid of plant life save for the occasional specimen of Sea Rocket (*Cakile edentulata*) or several other species. This is a high-energy environment strongly influenced by the effects of wind and salt spray, making it an extremely difficult habitat for most plants to survive in.

Prickly-pear Cactus

Back from the berm in the wind-blown accumulations of sand known as dunes, conditions become somewhat more hospitable for plant growth, and Dune Grass (*Ammophila breviligulata*) in particular colonizes these areas. Its network of rhizomes, or underground stems, stabilizes the dunes against the effects of wind and storms. However, the first dunes (foredunes) where Dune Grass occurs are still rather extreme environments and have low plant diversity.

On well-developed beaches, additional lines of dunes lie behind the foredunes. In protected spots plant diversity rises, and woody plants make their first appearance. Stunted dune forest develops in the most protected locations. These dune forests can be fantastic thickets of gnarled trees, vines and tangled underbrush. They can be home to northernmost populations of characteristically southern plant species.

In the generally quiet water environments of Long Island

Sound, beach development is, in contrast to oceanic beaches, more limited and vegetation zonation is less pronounced. The low dunes at Milford Point are densely covered over much of their extent by Dune Grass and its typical associates, Beach Pea (*Lathyrus maritimus*) and Seaside Goldenrod (*Solidago sempervirens*). These dune communities are comparatively fragile environments that suffer damage from foot traffic, so they are best observed from the berm.

Other plant species that inhabit area beaches include Spearscale (*Atriplex patula*), notable for its triangular leaves, Prickly-pear Cactus (*Opuntia compressa*) and Switchgrass (*Panicum virgatum*). The introduced but typical beach inhabitants Russian Thistle (*Salsola tragus)* and Wormwood (*Artemesia stellariana*) are also widespread. Moreover, the Southeastern native Yucca (*Yucca filamentosa*) sometimes escapes from cultivation onto Connecticut beaches. Although rare with us, the delicate, native Beach Heather (*Hudsonia tomentosa*) is found occasionally on area dunes.

Milford Point also possesses limited examples of dune thickets. Typical beach shrubs include Beach Plum (*Prunus maritima*), Bayberry (*Myrica pensylvanica*), High Tide Bush (*Iva frutescens*), Groundsel Tree (*Baccharus halmifolia*) and the introduced Beach Rose (*Rosa rugosa*). Although dune forest is not found on Connecticut beaches, scattered trees are present, particularly Eastern Redcedar (*Juniperus virginiana*), Black Cherry (*Prunus serotina*) and the introduced Tree-of-Heaven (*Ailanthus altissima*).

Wildlife: The beaches and adjacent waters of Long Island Sound are home to a diverse array of marine creatures. Shells of numerous mollusk species wash onto the beach where they are easily collected at the high tide line. Other species actually live in beach sand and may be found by digging.

Clam relatives present include the American Oyster (*Crassostrea virginica*), Bay Scallop (*Aquipecten irradians*), Blue Mussel (*Mytilus edulus*), Razor Clam (*Ensis directus*), Quahog (*Mercinaria*

mercinaria) and Soft-shelled Clam (*Mya arenaria*). An ecologically important but minute species, the fabulously abundant Gem Clam (*Gemma gemma*), is found on the bay side of beaches in fine sand and mud. It is notable for the deep amethyst spot present on its white shell.

Typical snail relatives that may be found on beaches include two large species of Moon Snails (*Lunatia heros* and *Polineces duplicatus*), a small Moon Snail (*L. triseriata*), the tiny Atlantic Oyster Drill (*Urosalpinx cinerea*) and the showy Channeled Whelk (*Busycon canaliculatum*). One of the commonest species found on Connecticut beaches is the Slipper Shell (*Crepidula fornicata*), named for its slipper shape. Two less common and smaller relatives, the Flat (*C. plana)* and Convex (*C. convexa)* Slipper Shells, also occur. A number of other mollusk species, including various minute ones, may be found on certain beaches.

In addition to mollusks, a variety of crab species are encountered at the beach. One common inhabitant is the Hermit Crab (*Pagarus longicarpus*), which occupies abandoned mollusk shells and may be seen running on the surface of the beach. Other common species is the Mole Crab (*Emerita talpoida*), and Lady Crab (*Ovalipes ocellatus*) which burrow into beach sand. Shells of the Spider Crab (*Libinia emarginata*), Rock Crab (*Cancer irroratus)* and Jonah Crab (*C. borealis*) may be found among beach debris (wrack) at the high tide line. Another smaller crab, *Neopanope texana*, is common among rocks and sand.

Reptiles and especially amphibians are largely absent from the beach. The highly saline environment is toxic to amphibians. An occasional Black Racer or Black Rat Snake might be found in sand dunes, but the most characteristic reptile inhabitant of the vicinity is the Eastern Diamondback Terrapin. This turtle lives in the adjacent saline waters and in tidal creeks, and comes onto the beach to lay its eggs in the sand.

Comparatively few bird species summer on beaches. Of

them, however, are two of Connecticut's most truly endangered: the Piping Plover and Least Tern. Both nest primarily in the sparsely vegetated sands of beaches. Because beach habitat has been overwhelmed by development here and elsewhere along the coast, there are few remaining areas available for breeding. Even within nesting areas, breeding birds can suffer high rates of nesting failure from a variety of sources, including predation by wild animals and

Least Tern nest

human-associated disturbance. Moreover, as populations become small and isolated like those of these species, random events like major storms can exert catastrophic influences on populations.

During my time in the Pacific, I observed the effects of random events on the Rota White-eye. A single typhoon that made landfall on the island eliminated several of the major remaining flocks. As there was no reservoir of birds from elsewhere to repopulate the vacated habitat, the effect of those losses was to push the species from dire status to nearly beyond hope. In the case of another critically endangered Pacific species, the Guam Flycatcher, once populations dropped below a certain point, they entered what was essentially free fall. In the language of mathematics, the slope of their population curve reached the point where time to extinction equaled zero. Within a matter of months, the species went from savable to extinct.

At seasons other than summer, a host of bird species occupy the beach, the adjacent tidal flats and even the air over the beach.

In the first category are various species of birds called sandpipers. The Sanderling is the most common of these, although even one of Connecticut's rarest fall migrants, the Baird's Sandpiper, can be found on beaches by persistent searching. The tidal flats are alive with sandpipers and other shorebirds in spring and fall, with species like the Greater Yellowlegs, Lesser Yellowlegs, Least Sandpiper, Semipalmated Sandpiper, Dunlin, Short-billed Dowitcher, Semipalmated Plover and Black-bellied Plover being among the more commonly encountered.

Migrant hawks and swallows may be seen flying over the beach primarily in fall. Among the hawks, the narrow-winged falcons like the American Kestrel and Merlin are generally earlier migrants, whereas the short, wide-winged accipiters, particularly the Sharp-shinned and Cooper's Hawks, are somewhat later migrants. The large and once critically endangered Peregrine Falcon also has again become a regular fall migrant along our coast. Even during my mid-November surveys of Milford Point made in preparation for writing this chapter, I found a Peregrine flying low over the beach as it headed west toward New York. Among the swallows, fall migrating Tree Swallows can build to impressive concentrations that move along beaches in flocks of thousands. Sometimes hawks will depart from their migration journey to prey upon swallows.

Some notable migrant landbird species also may be found among the dunes, with perhaps the most interesting being the Ipswich Sparrow. This well-marked subspecies of the Savannah Sparrow (long thought to be a distinct species) nests primarily on Sable Island, Nova Scotia, and trickles through our coastal area in fall. It is an exceptionally pale, sandy-colored bird that generally walks rather than hops (like most sparrows) among the dunes. Another interesting migrant sparrow that can be observed in dune grass and adjacent salt marsh is the Nelson's Sharp-tailed Sparrow, a close relative of our breeding Salt Marsh Sharp-tailed Sparrow. It differs from the latter in that it has blurry rather than sharply defined breast markings. Several other migrant land birds that are typical of beaches include the Snow Bunting, Water Pipit, Horned Lark and Lapland Longspur.

One of Connecticut's least known mammal species, the Least Shrew, has been recorded from beaches. Other typical mammalian inhabitants of beaches include the important predators of Least Tern and Piping Plover nests, the Striped Skunk and Raccoon. Meadow Voles also are frequent dune inhabitants.

Closing thoughts: The best beach in Connecticut is, unfortunately, not in Connecticut. The well-developed beach at Napatree Point is at the entrance to Stonington's Little Narragansett Bay, but is just across the state line into Rhode Island. It exhibits a more extensive area of dune thickets than most of Connecticut's beaches. It is also a magnet for rare migrant shorebirds and land birds. The only spring male Orange-crowned Warbler (a western species) that I am ever likely to see in New England was there singing from a perch in the dune thickets one May morning. I have also found such bird species as the Blue Grosbeak (a southern species), Ruff (a European shorebird), Parasitic Jaeger, Sooty Shearwater, Wilson's Petrel (all sea birds) and Snowy Owl (a rare migrant from the north) at Napatree Point.

The best beach that I have yet found for locating unusual mollusks in Connecticut is at Bluff Point State Park in Groton. A number of the smaller snail species may be found at the base of the beach and along the adjacent bluffs. Other beaches worth visiting include those at Hammonassett State Park, Clinton-Madison, Harkness State Park, Waterford, and Griswold Point Preserve, Old Lyme.

I also have a short Pacific postscript. In the years since I left the Pacific, Stan and I kept in touch for a time, but as our lives proceeded in diverging directions we drifted apart. This is a source of some significant regret, and it is still not uncommon for my mind to drift back to tropical afternoons, orchids, jungles, and the music of island birds. Sometimes I think also of the last day I spent with Stan. We had spent the morning freezing together on the island's perpetually fog-shrouded plateau, searching for flocks of white-eyes. We had come back to town for lunch, as we had done together many times. But on this occasion he insisted on buying me lunch. It was a simple thing, but Stan had a small income, and I had always avoided getting him into situations where he would have to spend money. But in this instance I knew what he was doing, and did not protest. Men are not so good with verbalizing emotions toward each other. He was telling me in the way that men do that I was his good friend.

Offshore Islands 18

Mount Agung forms the substance and soul of the island of Bali. It broods over the island at dawn, but then evaporates into tropical clouds until it again reveals itself in the sparkling stillness of another morning. It is Saturn, the bringer of old age, and Neptune, the mystic. It is placid, and verdant, and in an instant it is Mars, an inferno spewing rocks and toxic gas; a twin to its former neighbor Krakatoa. Agung is the cataclysmic destructor, and yet its black volcanic earth gives life to a bewildering profusion of beings.

The monumental slopes of Agung are ringed in rice paddies and cloaked in forest from tropical lowlands to dripping high elevation rainforest. These forests have been a source of fascination to naturalists, including Charles Darwin's peer, Alfred Russell Wallace. In the 19th century Wallace stared from the mountain's slopes, from forests filled with chickadees and woodpeckers, across a narrow channel toward the island of Lombock, where there were instead Lyrebirds and Megapodes. It was as if the Gods had drawn a line between these islands, separating the regions on either side into distinct realms. Wallace realized here that the Earth was indeed divisible into biological regions, and with this insight gave birth to the discipline of biogeography, the study of the historical development of the world's biotas.

It is said that tropical islands beguile forever their visitors, and to this I can attest. I can at any time close my eyes and instantly transport myself back to the slopes of Agung, smell its rainforest, stand among the waving fronds of its tree ferns. The passage of time exerts no effect on its hold. I found it a place in which I could be entirely seduced, but yet be forced to ponder how this languid giant could be an author of such doom. It is in its very nature a place that forces intense thought. I first understood on Agung how Wallace developed his insight, and I found the mountain led me to insights of my own.

I thought of those achievements we refer to as genius, those inspired thoughts that lead to revolutions in science, and realized they are less feats of intellect than they are the culmination of focused effort. As I stood also looking toward Lombock, Wallace's conclusions seemed inescapable. He had reached his momentous insight not because he was more able than others, not because he was more profound, but because he was there. In the air of Agung, he could have concluded no other way.

So it is with islands. They elicit thought. They offer lessons. They are the places where insights clouded by the cacophony of the mainland can be better illuminated. So let us consider another such place:

Within the realm of remote, Sarigan is more so than Bali. No one lives there. It is a dead volcano, rising nearly vertically from the sea, and crowned by a plug of volcanic rock more impervious to weathering than its surrounding plateau. Off its southern shore in the Mariana archipelago is Anatahan, a sleeping but young

Sarigan

volcano, and to its north is Pagan, quite awake and actively erupting. Each of these islands has its own story, but Sarigan's exhibits important threads common to all islands. There are comparatively few species present on it. The absence of others is initially an enigma, until one realizes other species were once there, but have since died out. Indeed, most islands that have been studied, even those viewed as virtually pristine, have lost a staggering proportion of their original faunas, generally in excess of 50 percent.

At dawn on Sarigan the forests still ring with the songs of the Cardinal Honeyeater, more the color of our Scarlet Tanager than Cardinal. It has a fine, curved bill that fits neatly into the coconut palm flowers from which it actively feeds. Its lemon-lime voice, unlike its color, has no North American equivalent. The voices of the honeyeaters are joined in the tropical morning by the squealing duets of male and female Micronesian Megapodes, the shrieks of the fruit-eating, jungle-dwelling Micronesian Starling, and the incessant staccato of the Collared Kingfisher, but little else.

While I was on Sarigan, I witnessed the final throes of extirpation of one of its other remaining species. The White-throated Ground Dove is widespread and successful in the Marianas, but in days of intensive surveys I found but two on the entire island. My studies on other islands demonstrated that this dove used the ground and native forest understory for feeding. But on this island, burgeoning populations of introduced goats and pigs had virtually eliminated all life below the forest canopy. Native forest itself had become restricted to the most bouldery and inhospitable steep slopes where hoofed mammals were largely absent. The coconut palms that had replaced the forest were a bonanza for the fabulously abundant Cardinal Honeyeater, but they provided little food for the dove. The bird's habitat had been virtually eliminated, and its Sarigan population appeared to be following suit.

Disturbance on islands produces profound consequences. Islands do not endure well the hand of humanity. They have developed in isolation for millennia, so have become naïve, one might say, and have few defenses against the kinds of disruptions that human activities bring. Hunting, habitat destruction, introduced competitors, introduced predators, and exotic diseases have all decimated island communities. Despite Sarigan's remoteness and uninhabitability, fleeting visits by humans have been sufficient to yield catastrophic consequences for its entire ecosystem.

Remote oceanic islands are the most fragile of island environments, but all islands share aspects of this ecological weakness. In fact, one could make many of the same observations about Connecticut's islands that one can make for oceanic islands. Connecticut islands are, like their tropical counterparts, also fragile spots where the hand of humanity has wrought catastrophic change. Human disruption in the form of exotic species introductions, habitat destruction and disturbance of wildlife continue to be significant problems for local island communities. However, also like their faraway counterparts, our own islands offer opportunities to reflect, and to discover important facets of the natural world.

Connecticut's islands are small, but they are ancient environments born at the close of glacial times. Much of what occurs on them does so in isolation from the mainland (albeit less complete isolation than on oceanic islands). As with oceanic islands, animals like birds with good dispersal skills have easily colonized them, whereas less good dispersers like mammals and reptiles have had a more difficult time doing so. The infrequency of mammal and reptile predators in island environments has made Connecticut's islands uniquely safe environments particularly for certain kinds of nesting birds. Let us examine further what can be learned from these environments by visiting some:

FIELD TRIP
The Norwalk Islands, Norwalk

Directions: Mr. Billy, a white-haired and pot-bellied Caroline Islander, once told me how his grandfather taught him to canoe across a thousand miles of open ocean to some distant dot, using little more than the shape of wavelets. Reaching the Norwalk Islands is, fortunately, less of a feat than this, as they can be seen from the shore of Norwalk Harbor. Only some of these islands, Chimon, Sheffield and Goose Islands, are available for visiting. They are part of McKinney National Wildlife Refuge, and may be visited with a special permit, which must be obtained through the refuge office in Westbrook. Visitors are unlikely to be permitted access during the bird-breeding season.

Equipment: A boat is required to reach the Norwalk Islands. The Norwalk Seaport Association operates a U. S. Coast Guard approved ferryboat service to Sheffield Island from mid-June through Labor Day. The ferry can be boarded at the Seaport Dock adjacent to the Norwalk Maritime Aquarium. Seating is on first come, first served basis. Groups of 10 or more may make reservations in advance. Call the Norwalk Seaport Association or visit their website for information.

Mosquitoes and ticks are abundant at certain times of year, so long pants, socks, long sleeve shirts, hats and insect repellent are wise choices. Binoculars and field guides are also helpful. Guides are particularly useful for distinguishing the numerous species of marine invertebrates that may be found in this environment.

The habitat: The Norwalk Islands were formed about 17,500 years ago when retreating ice paused for a time along what it now Long Island Sound. The deposits of sand, rocks and gravel accumulated at the ice margin before the ice again began retreating north. Many of the islands of southern New England, such as Fishers Island, Block Island, and even Long Island are similarly covered by thick deposits of glacial debris.

The terrestrial vegetation of the Norwalk Islands may be divided into four principal communities: salt marsh, shorelines, low thickets and woodland. Much as in the Pacific, the natural communities have suffered greatly from human activity. All of the upland communities have been overrun with introduced weedy species, particularly Japanese Honeysuckle (*Lonicera japonica*), Morrow Honeysuckle (*Lonicera morrowi*), Asiatic Bittersweet (*Celastrus orbiculatus*), Multiflora Rose (*Rosa multiflora*) and Tree-of-heaven (*Ailanthus altissima*). Moreover, parts of the islands have been altered during previous human habitations.

The community of sandy and gravelly beaches includes such natives as Dune Grass (*Ammophila breviligulata*), Sea Rocket (*Cakile edentulata*), Beach Pea (*Lathyrus maritima*), Seaside Goldenrod (*Solidago sempervirens*), Switchgrass (*Panicum virgatum*), and the vines Poison Ivy (*Rhus radicans*) and Virginia Creeper (*Parthenocissus quinquefolia*). Thickets inland from the shore are vegetated by shrubby species like Bayberry (*Myrica pensylvanica*), Winged Sumac (*Rhus coppalina*), Smooth Sumac (*R. glabra*), Common Elder (*Sambucus canadensis*), and Pasture Rose (*Rosa carolina*). Areas of more mature woodland are limited in their extent, but include scattered large (to two feet in diameter) Black Cherry (*Prunus serotina*) and specimens of Tree-of-heaven, Sassafras (*Sassafras albidum*) and Hackberry (*Celtis occidentalis*). Moreover, over large areas vines such as Virginia Creeper, Asiatic Bittersweet,

Little Blue Heron

Japanese Honeysuckle and Blackberry (*Rubus allegheniensis*) predominate.

Although they are not in the plant kingdom, the marine algae form another group of photosynthetic organisms that are conspicuously present. A variety of species may be observed washed onto the wrack line of the shore or among the larger intertidal rocks. Some of the most common include the flat green sheets of the green algae *Ulva lactuca*, the rubbery *Codium fragile*, sometimes called Dead Man's Fingers, and the long, wide straps of the brown algae Kelp (*Laminaria agardhii*). The dissected forms of *Fucus vesiculosus* and *F. spiralis*, the more finely dissected *Ascophyllum nodosum*, and the leafy red algae Sea Lettuce (*Chondrus crispus*) are found attached to intertidal rocks. On the brown algae, air bladders may be observed to assist with floating in the water.

Wildlife: The beaches, rocks and gravelly shores of these islands are home to a diverse array of marine creatures. Shells of numerous mollusk species are easily collected at the shoreline and among intertidal rocks.

Clam relatives that I have recorded in this vicinity include the American Oyster (*Crassostrea virginica*), Bay Scallop (*Aquipecten irradians*), Blue Mussell (*Mytilus edulus*), Ribbed Mussel (*Geukensia demissa*), Razor Clam (*Ensis directus*), Quahog (*Mercinaria mercinaria*), Surf Clam (*Spisula solidissima*), Northern Cardita (*Cardita borealis*), False Angel Wing (*Petricola pholadiformis*) and Soft-shelled Clam (*Mya arenaria*). A number of other species are also likely to be present.

Typical snail relatives present include the Channeled Whelk (*Busycon canaliculatum*), Moon Snails (*Lunatia heros* and *Polineces duplicatus*), Nassarius Snail (*Nassarius trivittatus*) and Atlantic Oyster Drill (*Urosalpinx cinerea*). One of the commonest species throughout the coastal area is the Slipper Shell (*Crepidula fornicata*), named for its slipper shape. The smaller Flat (*C. plana)* and Convex (*C. convexa)* Slipper Shells are present as well.

In addition to mollusks, a variety of crab species may be found. These include the Hermit Crab (*Pagarus longicarpus*), which occupies abandoned mollusk shells and may be seen running on shoreline sand and gravel. Shells of the Blue Crab (*Callinecthes sapidus*), Green Crab (*Carcinus maenis*), Lady Crab (*Ovalipes ocellatus*), Spider Crab (*Libinia emarginata*), and Jonah Crab (*Cancer borealis*) may be found among debris at the high tide line. Horseshoe Crabs (*Limulus polyphemus*), which are actually distant spider relatives, also may be found at the shoreline, particularly during their spring egg-laying season when they congregate in the intertidal sand of beaches.

Among rocks, the Rock Crab (*C. irroratus)* may be found, along with the small crab *Neopanope texana*. Barnacles (*Balanus balanoides, B. eburneus*) and such snail relatives as the Atlantic Dogwinkle (*Thais lapillus*) and three species of periwinkles (*Littorina littorea, L. saxatilis* and *L. obtusata*) inhabit the surface of the rocks. The periwinkles exhibit a pattern of ecological zonation. The first is a generalist species, and may be found occupying much of the intertidal zone. The second species occurs in the upper intertidal zone, and the third is found in the lower intertidal zone. Starfish (*Aquipectan irradians*), which are related to marine creatures like sea urchins, also may be found among the rocks or washed onto gravelly beaches.

The careful observer will also note the calcified shells of tiny creatures attached to the leaves of algae. These are colonies of

organisms called Ectoprocts.
Some types are found attached
to the shells of crabs or mollusks.
They can be exceedingly difficult
to identify.

Great Egret

Among the most notable
of the animal species inhabiting
these and some other islands in
the region are the birds. Bird
species in need of protection
from reptile and mammal
predators find these places
particularly important for
nesting. They include what are
referred to as wading birds: the
herons, egrets and ibises, named
thus because they wade through
shallow water with their long legs.
These wading birds nest in multi-species colonies called heronries
(often incorrectly referred to as rookeries, which are colonies of a
European species of crow).

One of the largest heronries in Connecticut is present in the
Norwalk Islands. Breeders include species like the Snowy Egret,
Great Egret and Little Blue Heron, all of which travel from the
island to tidal marshes and creeks where they feed on fish.

Another nesting species is the Cattle Egret, an Old World
native that appears to have colonized the New World (and much of
the rest of the world) on its own. Unlike its marsh-feeding cousins,
the Cattle Egret is largely terrestrial. It derives its name from its
habit of standing on the backs of cattle. As cattle disturb insects
in a pasture, the egrets fly to the ground and capture them. The
Cattle Egret is the only bird species occurring in Connecticut that
also may be seen on tropical Pacific islands.

Also nesting on the Norwalk Islands are Black-crowned and Yellow-crowned Night Herons. Although both these species may be observed during the day, they feed extensively after dark. On moonlit nights their shadowy forms may be seen gliding along tidal creeks. At dusk, the flights of herons and egrets back to the heronry are countered by the departure of these nocturnal species. They provide an example of an important point I make in classrooms, which is that environments may be partitioned among species not only based on habitat or foods chosen, but also based on time.

One other notable wading bird appearing as a nester in the Norwalk Islands is the Glossy Ibis. This species was a rare visitor to New England in the 19th century. One of the first Connecticut specimens ever taken may still be seen in a display case at Wesleyan University. Although our other coastal herons hunt visually, the Glossy Ibis is tactile feeder. In other words, its uses the sense of touch to locate food with its strange, curved bill, which it probes into tidal creeks.

Gulls form a conspicuous part of the nesting bird fauna of the Norwalk islands. In 1976 I conservatively estimated that 2,000 Herring Gulls and another 70 Great Black-backed Gulls nested on the gravelly beaches of these islands, and counts made since then indicate a current statewide population of 3,000 nesting pairs of Herring Gulls. This is quite a switch from the 19th century, when both species were known primarily as winter residents. Their enormous range expansion was linked specifically to human activity, particularly the proliferation of open landfills, which provided an enormous food source for these scavenging species. Since the 1970s, control programs and the closure of area landfills have greatly reduced summer populations in some areas.

A small gull species that may occasionally breed in the vicinity of the Norwalk Islands is the Laughing Gull. It appears commonly in spring and late summer. Another species present is the Fish Crow, a small, hoarse-voiced coastal species. Moreover, the showy but rare shorebird, the American Oystercatcher, has nested in the Norwalk Islands, as has the fish-eating Double-crested Cormorant. Characteristic landbirds of the islands include the Red-winged Blackbird, Song Sparrow, Willow Flycatcher, Gray Catbird, Yellow Warbler, Common Yellowthroat and Mourning Dove.

Predatory mammals and reptiles are largely absent from these islands (although the tiny Northern Brown Snake has been collected there, and the Northern Diamondback Terrapin may be found in the surrounding waters), which make the islands far more attractive to vulnerable species like waders, whose nests are easily preyed upon. Small mammals like White-footed mice and Meadow Voles are likely present on the islands, but I have not conducted any trapping studies there.

Closing thoughts: Connecticut is generally poor in island habitats, although it has numerous small islands, and several in particular are important bird breeding areas. Many islands are privately owned or have restricted access, and require permission to visit. Sandy Point is an island beach in Little Narragansett Bay off Stonington that is partly in Connecticut but mostly in Rhode Island. Nesting gulls and terns are found there, and the beach-nesting American Oystercatcher is also a frequent inhabitant. Waterford Island is a rocky island off the coast of Waterford that can be observed from shore. In summer it has a nesting colony of Common and Roseate Terns. Menunketesuck Island, just off Westbrook, is a small deposit of glacial till that has a coastal thicket with native shrubs Bayberry (*Myrica pensylvanica*), Panicled Dogwood (*Cornus racemosa*), and Pasture Rose (*Rosa carolina*), and native vines Poison Ivy (*Rhus radicans*) and Virginia Creeper (*Parthenocissus quinquefolia*). During many summers it supports a colony of nesting Least Terns. Other rare coastal breeders, the Willet and American Oystercatcher, have nested on this island as well. The more remote Faulkner's Island off Guilford hosts one of Connecticut's most important tern colonies. Finally, the small

Thimble Islands are close to the coast of Guilford, but many have been ravaged by development.

One other postscript: visiting oceanic islands is now a receding part of my own past, although the fact that I have done so is always with me. With little prompting I can easily remove myself back to those places, such as Bali and Sarigan and every other island that now owns some part of me. Sometimes while laying partly conscious in the morning's first light, the calls of some distant woodpecker are still transformed in my mind to the notes of some far more exotic, and now far more distant, island species.

Successional Habitats 19

F*irenze e come un albero fiorito*. It means Florence is like a tree in flower. They are the opening words to a very favorite aria, from Giacomo Puccini's lesser-known opera *Gianni Schicchi*, which is set on a day in the year 1299 in the city of Florence. Firenze is a city for which the passage of time has mattered little for many centuries; it has elements of that immortality which the rest of us seek. It is also a city with an extended tradition of scientific discovery. It is the place where Galileo perfected his ideas of the sun-centered solar system, and the place as well where he completed his investigations on the laws of motion.

Such ideas as those developed by Galileo are difficult to digest, in part because they use archaic notation, but also because the ideas are great ones not meant to be assimilated easily. They are not fast food, but multi-course dining. The notion of the dynamic nature of habitats, that they change over time, and that what is observed today is not always what will be present are other examples of difficult thoughts. The principal issue as I see it is one of scale. The city of Florence, for example, is indeed one that has not changed much in centuries, yet over a larger interval it has changed greatly. In 1299, many of its most important edifices were yet to be constructed. The Renaissance was as yet a glimmer on the horizon. Before the Middle Ages, it had been a Roman habitation. Before that, it was a primitive village. Before that, advancing glaciers from the Alps threatened its future site.

Old growth Pitch Pine

Similar statements could be made about those very environments around us in Connecticut. People have lived here for the better part of 12,000 years, and have exerted profound impacts on the landscape nearly from the day they arrived. Before there were cities there were villages, and before villages there were the temporary dwellings of nomadic people. During these earliest days of occupation, Connecticut would have been unrecognizable to contemporary inhabitants. Spruces, firs and outposts of tundra vegetation would have still covered the landscape. Long Island Sound as well as extensive inland areas were freshwater lakes. Before human arrival, ice covered the entire region.

So, for natural systems there is no always. The North American environment has been a dynamic one for the life spans of many or even most of the species of plants and animals with which we are familiar. During these species' tenure, their distributions have ebbed and flowed with the evolving landscape. Hence, making decisions about things like conservation priorities is not as simple as considering solely what species inhabited our region at the time of first European contact. By that time, people had been actively modifying environments for thousands of years. Natural climatic fluctuations had been modifying environments long before that.

I have advanced the idea that conservation priorities must be established based on present conditions and, therefore, on what is practical. Grassland communities have, for example, come and gone from our region. At present, physical environmental conditions do not permit their extensive development. Our prevailing natural systems are forest communities. Hence, in developing a regional conservation scheme, I have advocated focusing on especially prevailing systems, and avoiding efforts directed at systems whose time in our region has passed. Because small-scale disturbance is an integral component of forest ecosystems (evidence of which is provided by the number of species that are specifically adapted to exploit these disturbed areas), I have also advocated that small-scale disturbance-related components of forest systems be part of conservation strategies.

In the following trip, I explore the consequences of disturbance under the heading of secondary succession, which can be defined as the sequence of habitat development that follows a disturbance. I also explore the initial colonization of bare mineral environments by living organisms under the heading of primary succession.

FIELD TRIP
Bear Mountain, Salisbury

Directions: Bear Mountain is most easily reached by traveling north on Rt. 41 to Mt. Riga State Park. The entrance to the park is on the left just before Fisher Pond. Park at the entrance parking lot, and take the Undermountain Trail (blue dot trail) to its junction with the Appalachian Trail (white dot trail). Turn right on the Appalachian Trail and head upslope to the summit of Bear Mountain.

Equipment: Hiking boots are strongly recommended for the hike of about three miles to the summit. Ticks are present at certain times of the year, so long pants, socks, long sleeve shirts, hats and insect repellent are also wise choices. Binoculars and field guides are helpful. The trails are rather steep in spots and quite rocky. Take special precautions on wet days to avoid slipping on the rocks.

The habitat: Undermountain Trail first traverses the slopes of Mount Riga. These slopes are cloaked in forest that is primarily deciduous. The lower slopes typically accumulate water and dissolved nutrients from the upper slopes and as such, plant species preferring moister and richer conditions are present more frequently there. Species like Sugar Maple (*Acer saccharum*), Striped Maple (*A. pensylvanicum*), American Beech (*Fagus grandifolia*), White Ash (*Fraxinus americana*), Northern Red Oak (*Quercus rubra*), Eastern Hemlock (*Tsuga canadensis*), Witch Hazel (*Hamamelis virginiana*) and Cinnamon Fern (*Osmunda cinnamomea*) are characteristic of these lower slopes.

From the steep lower slopes, the trail more gradually ascends, but then again becomes steep as the slopes of Bear Mountain are approached. On these upper regions, conditions are more dry and infertile, although apparently not extremely so. Northern Red Oak is joined increasingly by species like Pignut Hickory (*Carya glabra*) and White (*Q. alba*), Black (*Q. velutina*) and Scarlet Oak (*Q. coccinea*). An oak relative, American Chestnut (*Castanea dentata*), was once a common component of these drier forests, but chestnut blight has reduced it to saplings and root sprouts. In the forest understory, typical dry site shrubs like Huckleberry (*Gaylussacia baccata*) and herbs like Bracken Fern (*Pteridium aquilinum*) are present.

Secondary successional landscapes: The forests of the east slope vary from young to mature, being perhaps 40-90 years old. They, like virtually all of the forests of southern New England, may be referred to as secondary successional forests. This term refers to the development of plant communities after some episode of disturbance. Logging is a typical type of disturbance that local forest communities have experienced, including those of Bear Mountain. In areas that have been logged, reforestation can be rapid because certain species, particularly the oaks and hickories, can sprout from stumps. Such re-grown forests are often referred to as sprout hardwood forests. However, the actual evolution of a new forest involves phenomena other than simply the re-sprouting of trees.

The bare mineral soil exposed during logging operations is quickly colonized by a variety of annual weed species (plants that set seeds and die after one growing season). In subsequent years, perennial herbs such as goldenrods and grasses become established, as well as certain types of woody species that require direct sunlight and reproduce best in mineral soils. Among these woody species are certain types of trees often referred to as pioneer trees, because they are the first to colonize an area. In our region, Gray Birch (*Betula populifolia*), White Birch (*B. papyrifera*), Quaking Aspen (*Populus tremuloides*) and Bigtooth Aspen (*P. grandidentata*) are typical examples of pioneer trees. Even though such species may be comparatively short-lived, they do not necessarily disappear from the forest as it matures, although they do tend to become more uncommon. Eastern White Pine (*Pinus strobus*) is another species that can densely colonize a disturbed area, but it also can invade even mature oak-hickory forests. At present, all these species may be observed in the Bear Mountain forests.

In logged areas, pioneer trees are joined by those that have sprouted from stumps. Species referred to as intolerant, that is, they do not compete well with other tree species in the forest interior, also seed into these open areas. Oaks and white pines are among these, although both are more precisely referred to as moderately intolerant, as they can persist in mature forests, albeit at reduced densities.

Once a forest matures, typically in 150 years, some of the species that have formed the forest canopy begin declining in abundance. The seeds of such species may not germinate as well in the leaf litter of the mature forest, or their seedlings may not compete well with those of other species in the

Three-tooted Cinquefoil

shaded forest interior. Over time, shade tolerant species like Sugar Maple, American Beech, Yellow Birch and Eastern Hemlock begin to predominate.

At present in Connecticut, forests are maturing at a rate beyond that at which succession is being reversed through logging. Consequently, statewide measurements of forests have shown a long-term shift in composition from oaks and hickories toward more shade-tolerant species. In many of Connecticut's forests, examining the understory or sapling layer of the forest provides clear lessons in the evolution of forest composition. For example, in winter the persistent dead leaves of sapling American Beeches reveal strikingly the extent to which this species is invading regional forests.

Although the term has become less fashionable with plant ecologists in recent decades, old growth forests are referred to as climax forests, in that they reach a stage at which they are self-perpetuating. That is, the species in the forest canopy are capable of replacing themselves. Records of virgin tracts surviving long enough in Connecticut to be studied by early plant ecologists, such as one that persisted into the early 20ᵗʰ century in Colebrook, support this notion of climax forest. However, as with virtually everything in nature, how forests develop over time is rather more complex than this simple generalization.

Even in the absence of such generally human-associated activities as logging and forest fires (many eastern forests are thought to have been largely "fire proof" before the advent of humans), disturbance is a characteristic part of the forest ecosystem. I have observed the damaging effects of summer thunderstorms, winter ice, snow, windstorms, disease and insect pests on forest structure. Although extensive forest areas may escape significant disturbance for centuries, disturbance eventually opens the forest to earlier stages in the successional sequence. In short, we may expect that, even when they are undisturbed by people, the region's forests will represent a mosaic of forest successional stages.

Primary successional landscapes: After ascending the slopes of Bear Mountain, a distinctly different habitat appears. The thin soil and rocky ridge of the mountain supports a community of low, scrubby growth and stunted trees. The summit of the mountain is high enough that its average daily temperature is lower than on the slopes below, making the summit resemble in some regards the alpine environments found on the higher peaks of the Green Mountains further north.

The cold, windswept and rather extreme environment of the summit has as well numerous exposed rocky surfaces. On these, the process of primary succession is occurring. That is, these inorganic surfaces are being colonized and modified by living organisms. Such processes occur only very slowly. Much the same process occurred throughout the entire region after glacial ice melted, when a bare mineral environment appeared from beneath the ice. Even after the approximately 15,000 years since ice retreated from this peak, this process is still occurring.

Lichens form a conspicuous cover over the surfaces of these rocks. These plantlike forms are actually symbiotic (mutually beneficial) relationships between primitive organisms: a fungus and an algae, with the fungus providing a mechanism for nutrient absorption and the algae providing a mechanism for carrying on photosynthesis.

These colonizers alter their environment (the rock) through their life processes. The organic acids they produce accelerate weathering of the rock and the weathered remains contribute to a developing layer of soil. Biological plus mechanical weathering of rocks yields cracks into which soil accumulates. In these cracks, the first plants colonize. Much as just after glacial times, species more typical of the far north may be found on these high peaks. Three-toothed Cinquefoil (*Potentilla tridentata*) occurs fairly commonly in these high altitude cracks on this and other Berkshire peaks, although Bear Mountain is near its local range limit (it also occurs further south in the Appalachians).

In areas where primary succession has proceeded further, woody plants have colonized, and low thickets of shrubs and stunted trees have developed. Some of these, like the shrubby Mountain Azalea (*Rhododendron roseum*) are also characteristic of northern and high mountain environments. Some pioneer tree species like the White and Gray Birch are, not surprisingly, present as well. In more mature areas, species like Black Oak, Scarlet Oak, White Oak, Sassafras (*Sassafras albidum*), Huckleberry and Bracken Fern that are also in the adjacent lowlands are present. Perhaps most surprisingly, species more characteristic of the Atlantic coastal plain like Pitch Pine (*Pinus rigida*) and Scrub Oak (*Q. ilicifolia*) are abundant in some of the most exposed areas around the summit. Hence, the community is an incongruous assemblage of typically southern and northern-associated species.

The assemblage is best understood in terms of the individual ecology of the species. Although species like Pitch Pine and Scrub Oak are present abundantly at coastal plain environments on Cape Cod, Long Island and New Jersey, both also extend their range well into the north. Cold is not a limiting factor for them in southern New England; they are adapted for dry and sterile conditions within our climatic regime. Those conditions are present on coastal plain sands, and they are present also on rocky summits. Species like the Three-toothed Cinquefoil, on the other hand, appear to require the northern climate, and are rarely found outside of it. These conditions reach their southernmost extension locally on the high peaks of northwestern Connecticut. Hence, as could be said for most any community, it is composed of species with ecological tolerances that overlap.

A surprising possibility appears to exist for these high elevation habitats. In addition to exhibiting aspects of primary succession, other aspects of them may illustrate the concept of the climax community. The stunted trees of this area are likely to be much older than might be guessed. Careful study of nearby Mt. Everett in Massachusetts demonstrated that on this peak the scrubby pines and oaks were several hundred years old. In other words, they represent a virgin habitat much like the first explorers to the region would have seen. Although logging, charcoaling activities and agriculture have altered the face of virtually all of southern New England, at least some of the peaks in the Berkshire plateau appear to have escaped this fate. They may be thought of as representing the climax community that is possible on these summits given the local conditions of climate, soil moisture, soil structure and chemistry, associated nutrient levels, potential pool of colonizing species, and frequency of mechanical disturbance (via storms) of the system.

We cannot assume that all peaks escaped disturbance, however.

Poor forestry practices led to frequent forest fires in the 19th century, and such fires altered the ecology of other mountaintops. Evidence indicates, for example, that Mt. Monadnock in southern New Hampshire was once forested to the summit. Its present "alpine zone," containing some of the same species present on

Eastern Milk Snake

Bear Mt., is largely an artifact of bad forestry and subsequent forest fires. Moreover, the origin of scrubby growth on high peaks in the southern Appalachian Mountains is unclear. It may be natural, or it may be the consequence of grazing by sheep as long ago as the 18th century.

Wildlife: The kinds of animal species occupying various types of habitats in earlier stages of succession are distinctly different from those found in more mature habitats like forests. Evidence suggests that many of the species associated with younger and rather ephemeral stages of successional habitats possess adaptations as well for locating and exploiting new occurrences of such habitats. Particularly certain bird species appear capable of adjusting rapidly their entire continental distributions in response to changing habitat conditions.

Among reptiles, a notable example of a species associated with successional habitats is the Smooth Green Snake. It inhabits abandoned land that has been colonized by herbaceous plants, mountaintop scrub, and areas that have been colonized by patches of pioneer trees and shrubs (old fields). Other species like the Box Turtle, Eastern Milk Snake, Black Racer and Eastern Hognose Snake may be found in weedy, successional areas as well.

A number of bird species are largely restricted to successional habitats. Many of these use even small openings within forest habitat. Considering the frequency with which such disturbances occur, it was small wonder to me that when I conducted large-scale surveys of habitat use by Connecticut forest birds, I found a whole suite of species that occupied these forest openings. Such species are sometimes referred to as forest gap species, and include birds like the Least Flycatcher, American Redstart, Northern Oriole, Rose-breasted Grosbeak and Gray Catbird. Other species like the Blue-winged Warbler, Prairie Warbler, Indigo Bunting and Chestnut-sided Warbler are associated with larger areas of disturbance.

Today, as forest extent diminishes and, thus, the number of naturally disturbed areas diminishes, commercial forestry operations have to some degree taken the place of natural disturbance. Many of these forest gap species are now frequently associated with openings created by forestry operations. Heterogeneity is likely to have always been a feature of regional forests, and in order for the entire community to persist, such heterogeneity must continue to be an important aspect of forest structure.

In the scrub habitats atop the higher peaks in the Bear Mt. area, species like the Rufous-sided Towhee, Gray Catbird, Common Yellowthroat, Chestnut-sided Warbler, Purple Finch and Ruffed Grouse are typical inhabitants. The surrounding higher elevation forest is also a place to look for one of Connecticut's rarest summer residents, the Swainson's Thrush.

Mammal species often associated with earlier successional landscapes include the Meadow Vole, Meadow Jumping Mouse, Red Fox and Eastern Cottontail. Other species occurring in Northwest Connecticut that may be found in the maturing forests of Bear Mt. include the Northern Flying Squirrel, Deer Mouse and Woodland Jumping Mouse. The Fisher and Black Bear are firmly established in the woodlands of Northwest Connecticut as well.

Closing thoughts: With the exception of coastal sand dune communities, the closest naturally occurring habitats to grasslands in Connecticut are several types of marsh edge communities. One is the Switchgrass (*Panicum virgatum*) community that fringes many of our tidal marshes along the coast. More extensive examples of this community are found at Great Meadow, Essex and Lord's Cove, Lyme, although in both instances these areas are maintained through periodic mowing. Another community, that dominated by Reed Canary Grass (*Phalaris arundinacea*), also forms persistent borders of some freshwater marshes. Good examples may be seen at Wethersfield Meadows, Wethersfield, Wangunk Meadows, Portland, and Cromwell Meadows, Cromwell. Some of these communities are maintained by mowing as well, although some that I have been examining since the early 1970s have persisted with no apparent manipulation. Both Switchgrass and Reed Canary Grass communities are better termed marshes than grasslands, as they occupy wet, muck soils that are periodically inundated.

Other types of upland grassland habitats also may be found in Connecticut, although these are best termed early successional habitats, as they are not persistent without periodic mowing or burning. Little Bluestem (*Andropogon scoparius*) is a common grass of early stages of old-fields, particularly in dry, gravelly or sandy soils, but when left undisturbed it is invaded and eventually replaced by woody plants. An extensive example may be seen at the Putnam Heights green in Putnam, which has been kept as a bluestem meadow via mowing since the 18th century. Israel Putnam is said to have trained the Connecticut militia at this spot before bringing them to fight at Bunker Hill. The footprints of colonial era militia buildings are still present on this green.

Old-field communities are somewhat ephemeral, generally persisting for only 30 years before they mature to woodlands. Characteristic examples with pioneer tree species like Gray Birch, Quaking Aspen, Eastern Redcedar (*Juniperus virginiana*) and

Common Juniper (*J. communis*) that I began observing in the 1970s are now woodlands. The pioneer trees are still present, but have been overtopped by oaks and pines. Examples of old-field habitats may still be found commonly throughout the state, although their frequency and extent has been steadily declining as regional forests mature. As they decline in abundance, the role of commercial forestry operations becomes increasingly important in maintaining the elements of the forest wildlife community that occupies these habitats.

Another rocky summit worth visiting in Connecticut is Mt. Misery in Voluntown. Although not high enough to result in average temperature declines (in fact, smaller hills generally have warmer average conditions at the summit than in the surrounding valleys, into which heavier cold air sinks), its dry, rocky summit gives rise to a Pitch Pine-Scrub Oak community somewhat resembling that on Bear Mt. Still another interesting summit is at Furnace Brook State Park in Killingly, where the summit of its rocky hill has also developed a Pitch Pine community.

Traprock Ridges 20

My life flirted with ending shortly after it had begun when one day in the Watchung Mountains of New Jersey I dove into a pond. I was perhaps four. People were jumping from a diving board, so I decided to do something similar. Even now I can see the underwater vision of foaming divers breaking the water. Once engulfed by the pond I was aware I could no longer breathe, although I recall no fear. An instant later, a hand snatched me from the water, and at that point my memories fade.

The Watchung Mountains are part of a chain of ridges that extend north along the Hudson River as the Palisades. On one of those ridges, Aaron Burr dueled Alexander Hamilton, which did cost Hamilton his life. From the Palisades, the ridges turn east into the Connecticut Valley. They are not real mountains, but the hardness of their blue rocks contrasts so much with that of the surrounding red sandstones that over geologic time they emerged from the sandstones as steep hills.

Unlike the great majority of landscapes in the metropolitan New York City area, many of the traprock ridges have retained their original character. They are natural choices for parklands, as they frequently offer commanding views of the surrounding countryside. One such park, with its titanic oaks, maples and rocky slopes, was the closest wild landscape to my home. As a teenager my only option for visiting it was to walk a 12-mile round trip, which I did every chance I got, winter and summer. Once there I rarely saw anyone else, and instead slipped into a world of solitude and reflection, rare commodities in that region. Many of the thoughts I first developed while exploring those places remain cornerstones of a personal philosophy. They provided a starting point for an extended journey, and periodically I find that returning to the contemplations of that time help make the present more intelligible.

In this volume I mention repeatedly the paradox of time. Time progresses linearly in our reckoning, yet in our experience the time separating events is uncertain. I can, for example, recall every instant of a day when I first climbed the cliff of a traprock ridge to survey the surrounding countryside. The intervening time is quite irrelevant. While scrambling over rocks, I found my first Hercules' Club, a native tree with tropical leaves and giant spines. I found also the nest of a Brown Thrasher in a shrub clinging precariously to the cliff edge. It is still the only one I have found. I remember being scared by the steepness of the cliff, but decided I must conquer that fear if I wished to remain on the scientific path I envisioned lying before me.

But I remember especially the summit and the incongruous view below. I was perched at the edge of a wild landscape, looking down upon a sea of urbanization. Floating over the city was a flock of crows, which I found I saw clearly for the first time. They were native animals, attached to the world in which my feet were planted, but they were venturing into a new, unnatural world. Yet they remained above it, more rooted in lofty wildness than in the urbanization below.

Then there was a hot summer day. I had walked the five miles to the local ridge. I planned some quiet contemplation while walking two more miles through the park, and then five miles home. It was something I had done many times. But on this day there wafted through the shimmering heat the sounds of African drums. They were impossible to escape, and I found I could think only of them. It occurred to me that the drums were akin to bird song, to the chatter of the squirrels. They seemed natural extensions of our own voice. I imagined some distant time when frightened humans huddled around fires, comforting themselves with these signals to lions and hyenas that humans were there to stay.

My earliest field notes come from traprock ridges, as do my first attempts at landscape photography. I have images of snow swirls on frozen streams, decaying trunks of dead oaks, and October maples shining in afternoon sun. They remind me of still another realization made early, upon which my view has not altered: that aesthetics shares a connection with science.

To a great degree what we study in science is a natural outgrowth of our aesthetic sense. In physics it is the quest to find "the single, beautiful kernel of an idea that explains everything that ever was, and ever will be." For those of us less abstractly inclined, we may start by taking walks in the woods or by going bird watching because we find such things delightful. But our attraction to this beauty is likely also to arouse curiosity, and we quickly find ourselves asking questions that fall into the realm of science. Why do those trees we like so much grow only by a stream? Why is it that our favorite bird always occurs in flocks? For the profoundly curious, the questions become equally profound. Why are there so many types of species? Why do certain groups of species always appear together?

I suppose we all have our special place, where we can have our private thoughts, deal with as best we can our mortality, and decide what we will make of the time we have available. The blue-gray landscapes of traprock have often been that place for me. Writing the descriptions that follow has been much like visiting an old and well-loved friend.

FIELD TRIP
Penwood State Forest, Simsbury-Bloomfield

Directions: Go north on Route 10 through Avon Center until the junction of Route 185. Go right and follow the road about 1.5 miles until the sign for Penwood State Park appears on the right. Go into the parking lot, where several trails along the mountain begin. The easiest trail is the old paved road that heads straight up the mountain from the lot. Another old road heads off to the right along the edge of the park. Several hundred yards after the beginning of this second road, a trail marked with blue dots, the Metacomet Trail, takes off to the left into the forest. This trail provides more of a wilderness experience. Either provides a good view of the environment.

Equipment: I recommend long pants, socks, a hat and insect repellent for most any outing, particularly during tick and mosquito seasons. However, especially the old paved road is a very easy walk. Field guides, cameras and binoculars are also valuable, particularly the latter, as they help in appreciating the wide vistas of the Connecticut Valley visible from lookouts on the mountain.

The habitat: Traprock ridges develop soils with low acidity, and they often exhibit a richer flora than in surrounding forests. The lower slopes have forests bathed in nutrients and moisture derived from higher elevations, and may be particularly diverse. Areas near streams and wet spots may be diverse as well. However, as with most rocky summits in our region, the exposed, thin soils of the ridge top are usually dry, and are inhabited by species capable of tolerating dry conditions.

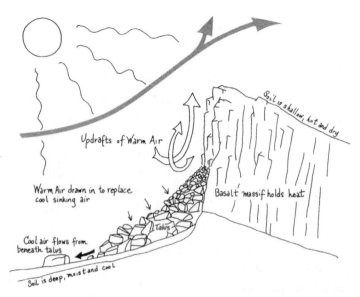

Updrafts of Warm Air

Warm Air drawn in to replace cool sinking air

Soil is shallow, hot and dry

Basalt massif holds heat

Talus

Cool air flows from beneath talus

Soil is deep, moist and cool

Courtesy, Connecticut Department of Environmental Protection

Another notable feature of traprock ridges is their talus slopes: steep slopes with piles of rocks that have fallen from vertical faces of cliffs. Talus slopes create several microenvironments due to the movement of air through them. Even though solar energy is absorbed by the talus, which can make the talus surface hot and dry, the surface also insulates the rocks below, keeping them cool. The cooler air among deeper rocks is comparatively dense and heavy, so it sinks through the talus and exits near the bottom of the slope. Warmer air enters the rocks to replace the exiting air, where it is in turn cooled. Hence, the climate at the bottom of the slope differs from that at the top, creating differing microhabitats for plants and animals.

Moister forests of traprock ridges are vegetated by a diverse assemblage of species, including Sugar Maple (*Acer saccharum*), White Ash (*Fraxinus americana*), Yellow Poplar (*Liriodendron tulipifera*), American Linden (*Tilia americana*), Northern Red Oak (*Quercus rubra*), Shagbark Hickory (*Carya ovata*), Yellow Birch

(*Betula lutea*) and American Beech (*Fagus grandifolia*). Some Eastern White Pine (*Pinus strobus*) is present, as are groves of Eastern Hemlock (*Tsuga canadensis*), although the latter is suffering mortality from Wooly Adelgid infestations. Toward drier ridge tops, Chestnut Oak (*Q. prinus*) becomes a common species, as does White Oak (*Q. alba*), Black Birch (*B. lenta*) and Red Maple (*A. rubrum*).

Characteristic understory shrubs and trees of traprock include Maple-leaf Viburnum (*Viburnum acerifolium*), Hophornbeam (*Ostrya virginiana*), Hornbeam (*Carpinus caroliniana*), Flowering Dogwood (*Cornus florida*), Witch Hazel (*Hamamelis virginiana*) and Mountain Laurel (*Kalmia latifolia*). Near cliff faces, Choke Cherry (*Prunus virginiana*) and Eastern Redcedar (*Juniperus viginiana*) may be common. Moreover, a characteristic coastal plain species found typically on sterile sand, the trailing shrub Bearberry (*Arctostaphylos uva-ursi*), sometimes appears on the rocky cliff edge.

The herbaceous flora of traprock contains a number of elements whose presence is related at least in part to neutral soil. A rich fern flora includes species like Rusty Woodsia (*Woodsia ilvensis*), Ebony Spleenwort (*Asplenium platyneuron*), Evergreen Wood Fern (*Dryopteris marginalis*), Lady Fern (*Athyrium filix-femina*), Maidenhair Fern (*Adiantum pedatum*) and Broad Beech Fern (*Thelypteris hexagonoptera*). Another notable herb is the geranium relative, Herb-Robert (*Geranium robertianum*), which can be abundant in moist, rocky spots.

Because the ridges are oriented north to south, they exhibit some latitudinal progression in plant species composition. A component of traprock forests to the south of Connecticut is Rhododendron (*Rhododendron maximum*), a common small tree of the central Appalachians, and an abundant species of the southern Appalachians. It is largely absent from Connecticut, although on occasion I have found apparent natives (it is planted as an ornamental, which makes determining the origin of individuals difficult) growing in the forests of southeastern, southwestern and even northwestern Connecticut. Strangely enough, it is also present locally in southern Rhode Island swamps and wet woods, a phenomenon that appears to be an artifact of glacial times.

Herb-Robert

Another straggler from the south that has been reported from traprock is Redbud (*Cercis canadensis*), another abundant small tree of the central and southern Appalachians. It is a showy, flowering species, like a number of Appalachian trees that don't quite make it to New England. It is widely cultivated in southern and central Connecticut, but survives cultivation in northern Connecticut only with difficulty. With us, it appears to grow as a native only extremely rarely, although even in these instances it may have escaped from cultivation. Appalachian species are replaced in Connecticut by shrubs and small trees with more northern affininties, like Striped Maple (*Acer pensylvanicum*), Mountain Maple (*A. spicatum*), and American Yew (*Taxus canadensis*).

Several elm relatives also may be found on traprock. For example, I have found Hackberry (*Celtis occidentalis*), growing from a cliff face, although with us it is also found near the coast, along major rivers, and on limestone.

Another enigmatic find from my explorations many years ago was a straight, tall (about 60 ft) elm I found growing on a forested slope. I knew it wasn't an American Elm (*Ulmus americana*), with its characteristic vase shape and habitat of riverbanks. It also didn't appear to be the often small tree of riverbanks and swamps, the Slippery Elm (*U. rubra*), although its asymmetrical, toothed leaves clearly identified it as an elm. I suspected it might be something I had never seen before: a Rock Elm (*U. thomasii*), which has been reported from eastern New York. I could reach no leaves or twigs to verify its identity, but the species is described as occurring in rich, moist, often limestone-derived soils. The neutral soils of traprock seemed to fit with this description reasonably well, so I was modestly confident I had identified it. In fact, I was elated; if correct it was a new species for me. Just as birdwatchers tally lists of birds they have seen, I kept lists of trees I had found.

But just as there is among birdwatchers the temptation to identify some flitting shape as a new species so that a "life list" may be lengthened, so I had likely fallen into the trap of wishful thinking, although it was not entirely clear I had done so until this year. In a recent exploration of Talcott Mountain, for the first time since my initial observation I found a tall, straight elm growing in upland traprock forest, but this time I could reach the leaves and examine the twigs. As soon as I touched the leaves my heart sunk. I knew what I had. The raspy surfaces of the leaves, combined with the weakly hairy buds told me I had found a particularly large and handsome Slippery Elm. My thoughts turned to that tree of many years earlier, and I knew I had solved an old mystery.

Wildlife: The first Box Turtle I ever found inhabited a place called Eagle Rock, New Jersey. The place, long since vacated by eagles, is a small traprock wilderness in a sea of suburbanization. How the species managed to persist in such a tiny island cut off from other populations is still remarkable to me. Box Turtles are, however, known from most Connecticut traprock ridges. Other characteristic traprock reptiles are two large species of black snakes, the Black Rat Snake and Black Racer. The poisonous Northern Copperhead is associated with traprock as well, particularly talus slopes. The first brook salamanders I ever found, the Northern

Dusky and Northern Two-lined salamanders, also came from a stream flowing through traprock. The two species are commonly found on our ridges.

Some of my most memorable experiences in bird watching have occurred on traprock ridges. To be sure, the observations were sometimes less about the habitats than because the places were islands of trees in a sea of urbanization. For example, every fall I note migrating Blue Jays working their way through my yard, but whenever I do I always think of an autumn day at a city park, when I saw not one flock, but flock, followed by flock, followed by flock of Blue Jays. Urban traprock parks are also still the only places I have ever seen the forest filled with *flocks* of spring male Scarlet Tanagers. I have seen similar urban extravaganzas by Palm Warblers, early spring migrants that more typically dribble through our area.

And then, of course, there is hawk migration. I have been present on traprock ridges on September days when the sky has appeared to erupt with thousands of Broad-winged Hawks flying past in a matter of an hour. I have also braved November winds to watch Goshawk after Goshawk drift by at eye level, staring directly at me with their blood-red eyes.

The north-south orientation of New England's traprock ridges, combined with the physics of air movement, creates conditions ideal for daytime migrants like hawks. From September to November each year, the skies over these ridges fill with hawks on their way south. On days when cold fronts push down from the north, hawks may migrate in particularly large numbers. The typical progression of fall migration is Broad-winged Hawks, Kestrels and Merlins in September, Sharp-shinned and Cooper's Hawks in October, and Goshawks and Bald Eagles in November. Eagles continue to trickle through in December, and the very fortunate may sight a rare Golden Eagle at this time.

The north-south traprock ridges intercept winds and create

cushioning updrafts along their length. Moreover, as land heats air just above it during the day, cells of warm air (referred to as thermals) rise along the ridges. Hawks make use of these phenomena. The characteristic fall occurrence of hawk "kettles," a swirling bubble of birds, is a consequence of birds using thermals. Once birds ascend in a thermal, they leave it and glide down to a lower elevation where they may encounter more rising air. Biophysicists refer to the glide as passive (non-powered) flight, which requires comparatively fewer calories than active (flapping) flight. Engaging in behaviors like these significantly reduces the energy required by hawks to make the daunting migration journey, which brings some species all the way to the tropics.

Unlike the birds, there are no obviously remarkable characteristics of the traprock mammal fauna of which I am aware. In field observations on traprock and in live trapping studies I have performed in nearby forested lowlands, I found the same type of species (e.g. Gray Squirrel, Red Squirrel, Southern Flying Squirrel, Chipmunk, White-footed Mouse, Pine Vole, Short-tailed Shrew) present in many upland forests. However, comparing population densities of species on traprock with those of other forest habitats might prove revealing.

Although the notion that linear tracts of natural habitat serve as corridors for wildlife dispersal is not applicable to all species, the forested north-south corridors of traprock may serve that purpose for certain mammals. Traprock ridges are becoming isolated from other natural areas as the Connecticut Valley develops, so may come to assume an increasingly important role in mammal dispersal.

Closing thoughts: A number of Connecticut's traprock ridges have pubic hiking trails through them, even those in private ownership. Places like West Rock, New Haven, Pistapaug Mountain, Durham, Lamentation Mt., Meriden, Higby Mt., Middlefield-Middletown, West Hartford Reservoir, West Hartford, and Talcott Mt., Bloomfield, are all accessible to hikers.

Calcareous Habitats 20

An autumn rain pelted without letup while I conducted reconnaissance for this chapter. It was the day I had to explore the area, so I endured the weather and did what I had to do. I dread spending days like that, perhaps as much as all the other animals who have little choice about being outside, but such is the nature of nature. This realm is an often hard place in which to exist, but regardless of the extreme, animals eat or die, plants survive or not. I think on such days of Ernest Thompson Seton, the 19th century naturalist who once wrote, "There are no happy endings in nature."

The natural world is indeed a harsher place than we indoor beings might presume. I have tasted this, because I have sometimes had to explore it at its worst in order to discover what happens during such times. I have discovered, for example, that even at wind chills of –45°F, birds are out and about actively feeding. During super-typhoons, the strongest storms the atmosphere can generate, tropical trees drop branches in such a way that within days these fallen branches begin to sprout leaves and send down roots. During daylong downpours, birds may be stationary for a time, but ultimately they resume their feeding, albeit so secretively that finding them is a challenge.

But there is more to be gleaned from observing the natural world in all its states than solely that it is a harder place than we might wish. There is a mirror image to this hardness, and in the reflection we see not cruelty, but instead a manner of beauty that is not otherwise present. These can be monochrome times; times of glistening raindrops dripping from leaves in sheets of silver. They are the times when I most wish to reach for my camera, when the landscape reveals the depth of its character.

I was reminded during the dreariness of my limestone swamp explorations of an interview I gave some years ago. The issue arose, why should wild places be preserved? I proposed that nothing traditionally advanced as a reason for conserving really had much to do with our motivation. All the traditional arguments might be true enough, i.e. economic value, medical value, etc., but none were the fundamental underlying force. Our reasons instead had to do with the aesthetic. It was as if we were afraid to admit this, as if it somehow weakened our case. I believed otherwise.

I argued that we want to preserve tracts of wildness because we find them beautiful. I pointed out that we are not alone in this sense of aesthetic. Even Chimpanzees are said to stand awestruck at the sight of a colorful sunset. It is something that we might think of as having its origins in responses so humble as the attraction of insects to flowers. It is one of our senses, like hearing or seeing. We require air to breathe, and beauty to behold. It is the driving force that brings us to create music, and art, and literature. We cannot separate our humanness from this need.

And beauty is born not simply of sunny warmth. It reaches its zenith in the drama of an approaching storm, in the hoarfrost of a white morning so cold that the atmosphere has wrung itself free of moisture. It is to be found in the groaning branches of the wind-whipped tree, and in the turquoise fountains of ice draping a wind-battered cliff. We are products of the same natural world that produces these visions. We respond to them as instinctively as we do to food. They are moods as we have moods, and with them we are intertwined.

River ice

Several years ago at a conference on endangered birds, I argued similarly that our interest in conservation of the creatures that populate these wild landscapes had less to do with practical values of conservation than our sense of aesthetic. I spoke about a group of birds called white-eyes that inhabit remote islands:

"In order to survive, every endangered species may need a champion, but why bother? This is the unpleasant question that most of us consciously or unconsciously avoid, or choose instead to hide behind transparently weak dogma when we must think about it. Do we really believe that a few hundred tiny birds on some remote dot might hold the key to ecosystem stability? How many of us believe that within the bodies of white-eyes lies the undiscovered chemical that will cure all the ills of mankind? So why do we do it?

Probably like some of you, I am a great fan of music. For some peculiar reason, probably related to the reason that I so adore little green birds, I love especially rather obscure compositions like

Handel's operas. Now, despite the fact that about as many people listen to these operas as have seen Rota White-eyes, it has occurred to me that if the last page of the last copy of one these operas were lost, it would break my heart. Popular or not, these works define our humanity. Their creation testifies to our sense of the aesthetic, of our capacity for being moved by the sublime. Intelligent, bright-eyed little beings like these birds, so filled with their exuberance for life, quite fall within the realm of the aesthetic. Certainly the loss of any of these beings, who first conceived of melody and harmony, of counterpoint and fugue, would also be far more than enough to break my and likely your hearts. I do not think we need to look further for reasons to protect them."

So, as I argue for why natural landscapes and their components should be preserved, I argue that aesthetics alone is the key reason for why we wish to do so, and this fact is sufficient justification for carrying out conservation measures. If we were to conclude otherwise, then we must also question our museums and galleries and concert halls. We need there to be a beautiful world if in it our souls are to persist. With souls excised, how long can we continue before we wither into the same emptiness as that which surrounds our tiny planet?

The field trip that follows concerns environments that develop on calcareous (limestone and marble) rocks. It would be reasonable to say that I have saved the best for last.

Maidenhair Spleenwort

The natural environments that develop on these rocks derive quite literally from the skeletons of preexisting life. All calcareous rocks are the descendents of ancient coral reefs, and these rocks erode to a rich soil that supports perhaps the most interesting of our native floras. Within the realm of the aesthetic, much can be found here that falls within this definition.

FIELD TRIP
Robbins Swamp, Salisbury & Canaan Mt., N. Canaan

Directions: The easiest way to view Robbins Swamp is to travel north on Rt. 126 in Salisbury. At several spots the road approaches a railroad grade very closely, and it is possible to stand near the railroad embankment (these tracks are still in use, so exercise caution) and look down at the swamp. Marked parking areas are also present on Rt. 126 and on Rt. 7, although no established trails are present for hiking into the swamp.

A good place to view the calcareous uplands of Canaan Mt. is along Lower Rd. in North Canaan. This road may be reached by traveling west on Rt. 44 to the junction of Lower Rd. in East Canaan village. Housatonic State Forest (Canaan Mt.) borders this road, although there are again no established hiking trails to follow in this area. Other parts of Canaan Mt. on Rt. 7 do have hiking trails, although I have not observed calcareous exposures along them.

Equipment: Trails are few in these areas, so proper field gear is valuable in negotiating the area. Robbins Swamp is largely too wet to traverse without rubber boots, and in any event is difficult to travel through. Ticks are present during much of the year, and black flies and mosquitoes can be ferocious into early summer, so long pants, socks, long sleeve shirts, hats and insect repellent are wise choices. Binoculars and field guides are helpful. Canaan Mt. is steep and quite rocky, so if you choose to explore it take special precautions to avoid injury. During the hunting season, the area should be avoided during peak hunting hours (early morning and late afternoon). I recommend that orange reflective clothing be worn during this season.

The habitat: Robbins Swamp is one of the largest freshwater wetlands in Connecticut. It is variously an open swamp with scattered trees and a closed one where the forest canopy is dense. Calcareous rocks underlie it, so its physical environment is uncharacteristically rich and low in acidity.

Much of Robbins Swamp is forested by trees that would be familiar in any swamp. The commonest tree species present include Red Maple (*Acer rubrum*) and Yellow Birch (*Betula lutea*), but others like Eastern White Pine (*Pinus strobus*), Eastern Hemlock (*Tsuga canadensis*), Swamp White Oak (*Quercus bicolor*), Black Ash (*Fraxinus nigra*) and Green Ash (*F. pennsylvanica*) are also widespread.

Another species present locally is the deciduous conifer Tamarack (*Larix laricina*). It is primarily a species of the far north, where it inhabits swamps and bogs. With us, it is most widespread in northwestern Connecticut, but it occurs as well in northeastern Connecticut, and I have found it even in bogs of the northern Connecticut River Valley.

A species sometimes found growing in association with Tamarack is Northern White-cedar (*Thuja occidentalis*). It occurs in wet areas and uplands where it prefers calcareous soils, but it inhabits acidic locations as well. I have found it growing near Robbins Swamp on marble ridges and at the edges of bogs. It is also a commonly planted and escaped ornamental, so knowing which individuals are native and which are introduced is problematic. The species is a peculiar one in that it is primarily a tree of the far north, although it also grows along rivers in lower elevations of the southern Appalachians in climates that are milder than here.

A tree found with us only in the limestone soils of western Connecticut is the Bur Oak (*Quercus macrocarpa*), which is present at swamp borders and also in upland areas. It is a large and handsome tree, superficially like White Oak (*Q. alba*), but with leaves that appear to be divided into an upper and lower half. The tree's name is derived from the cap of its acorn, which is rough and wiry like the kind of burs that get caught in the fur of pets. Another oak of calcareous uplands is the Yellow Oak (*Q. prinoides muhlenbergii*), a distinct tree-like form of the usually scrubby Chinkapin Oak of the Connecticut shoreline and sand plain areas. Hackberry (*Celtis occidentalis*), a relative of the elms that is a floodplain and coastal species, also reappears in calcareous upland areas.

Another tree that I have not had success finding in Connecticut, although I have found it in adjacent eastern New York, is the Black Maple (*A. nigrum*). It should be present in the limestone valleys of western Connecticut, as it is more of a river bottom tree than its close relative Sugar Maple (*A. saccharum*). However, it is known to hybridize rampantly with Sugar Maple, so distinguishing individuals may prove difficult in our area. Some authorities consider Black Maple to be a variety of Sugar Maple, although the bark and leaves of typical trees are quite distinct.

The understory of swamps is characteristically dense, in part because shallow-rooted swamp trees tend to fall over and leave gaps in the swamp canopy. Common species include Winterberry (*Ilex verticillata*), Highbush Blueberry (*Vaccinium corymbosum*), Witherod (*Viburnum cassinoides*), Arrowwood (*V. recognitum*), Spicebush (*Lindera benzoin*), Mountain Holly (*Nemopanthus mucronata*), Speckled Alder (*Alnus rugosa*), Sweet Pepperbush (*Clethra alnifolia*), Swamp Azalea (*Rhododendron viscosum*), Pink Azalea (*R. nudiflorum*) and Mountain Laurel (*Kalmia latifolia*).

A less widespread viburnum that occurs at the edges of swamps primarily in northwestern Connecticut is Highbush Cranberry (*V. opulus*). Its clusters of red fruits and three-pointed leaves make it a particularly attractive viburnum. Another shrubby species present in (although not restricted to) wetter calcareous areas of western Connecticut is Prickly-ash (*Zanthoxylum americanum*), a spiny species that can produce dense thickets.

The common herbaceous species inhabiting Robbins Swamp are similar to those found in any swamp. Ferns are a particularly abundant component, and include Cinnamon (*Osmunda cinnamomea*), Royal (*O. regalis*), and Sensitive (*Onoclea sensibilis*) ferns. Other common herbaceous species include the large-leaved Skunk Cabbage (*Symplocarpus foetidus*) and similarly large-leaved False Hellebore (*Veratrum viride*).

A notable feature of calcareous swamps is that certain species are unusually widespread in such areas. A number of these are not particularly exciting or easily identifiable, like sedges and pondweeds, but others are quite showy. One, for example, is a relative of the familiar Pink Lady's Slipper (*Cypripedium acaule*) of acidic soils. This species, the Yellow Lady's Slipper (*C. calceolus*), is often instead an inhabitant of calcareous swamps. It is locally common in area swamps.

One of the most distinctive features of upland calcareous areas, such as those present in part of the Canaan Mt. area, is the rich fern flora. Some ferns are largely restricted to this habitat, like the delicate Maidenhair Spleenwort (*Asplenium trichomanes*), Bulbet Fern (*Cystopteris bulbifera*) and Purple-stemmed Cliffbrake (*Pellaea atropurpurea*). Others, like the Ebony Spleenwort (*A. platyneuron*), Oak Fern (*Gymnocarpium dryopteris*), Blunt-lobed Woodsia (*Woodsia obtusa*), Narrow Beech Fern (*Thelypteris phegopteris*), Broad Beech Fern (*T. hexagonoptera*), Ostrich Fern (*Matteucia struthiopteris*), and Rattlesnake Fern (*Botrychium virginianum*), are widespread in this habitat but not restricted to it. A "fern ally", the Variegated Horsetail (*Equisetum variegatum*) is also present in calcareous mud, along with rarer species of horsetails.

Other typical herbaceous plants of rich soils, such as those of calcareous uplands, include a number of showy species

Canada Warbler

like Foamflower (*Tiarella cordifolia*), Twisted Stalk (*Streptopus amplexifolius*) and Mitrewort (*Mitella diphylla*). Other handsome species present include Blue Cohosh (*Caulophyllum thalictroides*), Herb-robert (*Geranium robertianum*), Red Baneberry (*Actea rubra*) and White Baneberry (*A. alba*).

Wildlife: Many of the reptile and amphibian species typically found in swamps and rich upland forests also can be expected to be present in calcareous areas. In Connecticut, one reptile species, the rare and secretive Bog Turtle, traditionally has been associated with calcareous swamps. Elsewhere in its range it is not restricted to calcareous habitats, however, suggesting that this apparent habitat preference may be in part an artifact of its geographic distribution. It is present only in far western Connecticut, and this same region is where calcareous wetlands are found.

Among snake species, the Northern Redbelly Snake is more likely to be encountered in northwestern Connecticut, although it is not restricted in occurrence to calcareous soils or to this region. Among salamander species, the Jefferson's Salamander is found solely in western Connecticut, including the Canaan Mt. area. Its close relative, the Blue-spotted Salamander, is known from the vicinity but it also occurs locally in eastern Connecticut.

Bird life in the more open portions of Robbins Swamp is characterized by species like the Common Yellowthroat, Yellow Warbler, Gray Catbird, Ruby-throated Hummingbird and Swamp Sparrow. The Nashville Warbler, a northern species near its southern range limit, is on occasion found in area swamps like this one. I have also found the more northerly distributed Yellow-bellied Sapsucker inhabiting more open portions of swamps in this region.

In heavily forested sections of the swamp, particularly where conifers are present and shrubbery is dense, the Northern Waterthrush and Canada Warbler are regular summer inhabitants. The black-necklaced Canada Warbler is reasonably obliging in terms of allowing itself to be seen, but only patience will permit an observer to gain a glimpse of the secretive Northern Waterthrush. Another species that may occur in conifer-dominated swamps is the Winter Wren, particularly where the swamp borders rocky, conifer-clad slopes. Moreover, the Red-shouldered Hawk is often associated with swampy environments, and when present it is usually easy to find because it calls loudly and persistently.

In the upland environments of Canaan Mt., the Nashville Warbler is again found, this time inhabiting forest openings and old fields where conifers are present. It is joined in these habitats by several other northerly-distributed species, including the Least Flycatcher and Magnolia, Chestnut-sided and Golden-winged warblers. In mature forests where white pines and hemlocks form an important portion of the canopy, still more species of northern affinities may be found. The Red-breasted Nuthatch, Dark-eyed Junco, Blue-headed Vireo and Blackburnian, Black-throated Green, Black-throated Blue and Yellow-rumped warblers are all present, and in drier areas they are joined by the Hermit Thrush. In mature deciduous forests, I have also found the rather rare Cerulean Warbler. One other northern and western-associated species, the Common Raven, has moved into the Canaan Mt. area in recent years, and its loud, hoarse calls usually make it easy to find.

Mammals of the Canaan Mt.-Robbins Swamp area include several species with northern and western affinities. The Deer Mouse, a close and nearly indistinguishable relative of the familiar White-footed Mouse, approaches its eastern range limit in western Connecticut. The Northern Flying Squirrel, the boreal cousin of the widespread Southern Flying Squirrel, is also largely restricted to hills of northern Connecticut. Furthermore, the Fisher has ranged south into Connecticut in the past few decades. The Fisher's more widespread cousins, the River Otter and Mink, may be found in the Robbins Swamp area, along with the swamp and bog-dwelling Southern Bog Lemming and Red-backed Vole. Still another northern species present in the region is the Snowshoe Hare. Although I have found it to be common and conspicuous further north, I have had little success finding it in northwestern Connecticut.

Closing thoughts: A superb spot for seeing the flora of calcareous habitats is just a short distance away from Robbins Swamp at Bartholomew's Cobble, which is just across the Connecticut border in Massachusetts.

*The author, Robert Craig, pictured
with the artist, Barbara Lussier.*